SHARED BURDENS

SHARED BURDENS

SUE V. SCHLABACH
GLEN A. ROTH

Good Books®

INTERCOURSE, PA 17534

IN COOPERATION WITH SHARING PROGRAMS

Shared Burdens is published in cooperation with Sharing Programs. Sharing Programs is a church-related organization available to persons who are part of the Mennonite family of churches. The Plans operated by Sharing Programs provide a means for sharing together in fire and storm losses to property, and liability and medical obligations related to the operation of motor vehicles (motor vehicle plan participation is limited to Pennsylvania). Sharing Programs cooperates with other Mennonite church-related sharing organizations in attempting to meet the needs of its members.

Many of the stories in *Shared Burdens* lend themselves to study and discussion in small groups, retreats, or Sunday school classes. A list of study questions is available upon request by calling or writing:

Glen A. Roth
P.O. Box, 10367
Lancaster, PA 17605
Telephone: 800/222-2455 or 717/293-7100
Please send $1.00 for postage and handling. Thank you.

Design by Dawn J. Ranck

Cover artwork—"Shared Burdens," carved drawing on a clay tile,
by Sandy Zeiset Richardson.

SHARED BURDENS
Copyright © 1993 by Good Books, Intercourse, PA 17534
International Standard Book Number: 1-56148-100-9
Library of Congress Catalog Card Number:

Library of Congress Cataloging-in-Publication

Shared burdens / [compiled by Sue V. Schlabach, Glen A. Roth].
    p. cm.
    Includes indes.
    ISBN 1-56148-100-9 : $6.95
    1. Caring—Religious aspects—Christianity—Case studies.
2. Mennonites—Charities—Case studies. I. Schlabach, Sue V.
II. Roth, Glen A.
BX8128.W4S53   1993
261.8'32'088287--dc20   93-38443
                               CIP

For true evangelical faith is of such nature that it
cannot lie dormant.
It seeks and serves God.
It clothes the naked.
It feeds the hungry.
It comforts the sorrowful.
It shelters the destitute.
It aids and consoles the sad.
It returns good for evil.
It serves those that harm it.
It prays for those who persecute it.
It seeks that which is lost.
It binds up that which is wounded.
It heals that which is diseased.
It has become all things to all people.

—excerpted from
Why I Do Not Cease Teaching and Writing,
Menno Simons, 1539

Table of Contents

WHOSE STORIES ARE THESE?

Now that comparatively few Mennonites are self-employed, how can they respond when a fellow church member is faced with a crisis and needs their help?

Today, when many Menonite women are employed outside their homes, who will go when a neighbor is suddenly in need?

Is this faith community resourceful enough to bring relief to the newer varieties of "trouble"—those brought on by dysfunctional families, medical advances that extend life but don't remove the need for care, urban crises of poverty, racial tensions, violence?

Mennonites have been distinguished by a particular practice since their beginnings—the unconditional offer of aid and assistance when trouble strikes a member. Commonly known as "mutual aid," the practice has traditionally expressed itself in barn raisings, in the community's providing ongoing care for a disabled individual, in their paying bills when a breadwinner has lost employment.

What happens when the impulse to serve or care for another is no longer "practical"?

This collection of stories was gathered from contemporary Mennonites, a Christian group sometimes known as Anabaptists, who trace their roots to the radical Reformation of the early sixteenth century. They began, by fits and starts, more than 450 years ago and have, through the centuries, weathered persecution, many migrations, economic difficulties, occasional muddling of the vision, and always the temptation to accommodate to the prevailing society. Yet their commitment to live as faithful followers of Christ, within a community that nurtures their spiritual lives and supports them in right living, has allowed them to continue and even grow, although modestly.

Marked from the beginning by their conviction that one's faith will be expressed in one's life, Mennonites have always struggled to live the love that Jesus taught. Caring for each other within the community of faith has been a distinguishing quality of these people. Certain of these practices have become well known—barn raisings, sewing circles, and the formation of relief organizations like Mennonite Central Committee and Mennonite Disaster Service, and a number of aid and insurance programs.

But time and the surrounding world have affected the Mennonites. Many are now professionals without the flexibility and time available to respond quickly to a sudden casualty. Today, more than in the past, it is difficult to help sufferers with prolonged illnesses because volunteers need to return to their jobs. Many members do not live as close to each other as they once did, so they may not even know of another's need. Complicating ethical issues also intervene—how, for example, should a congregation care for a member couple who divorces, when the church has traditionally forbidden divorce? How does a faith community express care when one of its own is depressed or abused or sidelined because of gender? Can an urban congregation do anything to dent the vast needs of its members who bring racial, economic, and educational terrors with them?

Will the children and young people of the church know, as certainly as their parents did, about this essential part of being faithful Christians? Will they have the impulse to offer themselves, as well as the resource, the imagination, and the willingness that inspired their foreparents, who tried to follow the example of Jesus?

The idea of writing a book about current caring practices and dilemmas among Mennonites grew out of an effort by my [Glen's] employer, Sharing Programs, to encourage children to learn about caring for one another. A few years ago, Sharing Programs sponsored an essay contest. Students, ages eight to 18 from 16 Mennonite schools in Pennsylvania, submitted over 600 essays about caring. I was overwhelmed by this wealth of untold stories. These were not only about barn raisings and making meals, but about prayer vigils and chemotherapy. People touching people in times of need.

I was deeply moved by what we received from the students and thought there should be a way to tell these stories more widely. So, with the blessing of the Sharing Programs leadership team, I began to conduct interviews and gather stories from Mennonite people across North America.

When Sue Schlabach joined the Sharing Programs staff, we conducted interviews together. With each interview we became more and more impressed that careful and empathetic listening is a way of sharing burdens.

Helping to bear another's burdens was an attitude I [Sue] absorbed almost unconsciously as a child. When I was 10 years old, my friend Marjorie and I had a talk about our extended families. Marjorie was a friend from church, and we loved to spend Sunday afternoons making up stories together. That day we were looking for material for a new plot. I remember her telling me about the financial hardships that plagued some of her ancestors. I responded, "Didn't their church help them?" Marjorie told me her family members weren't part of a church and had no one to help them. I was shocked. Already I felt a sense of security in my church family. If something terrible happened to me, I was reassured that I would be taken care of. Until then, I thought everyone else had a similar support network.

As I got older, I continued to see evidence in my church that my security was warranted. There truly was a network in place. I could see the members making a genuine effort to love and help each other. When I later visited and participated in several other Mennonite churches, I learned that not all functioned as well as my home congregation. I was grateful for that nurturing environment which made me proud to be part of the Mennonite church.

Together we have learned in a startlingly clear way that listening is itself a powerful act of mutual aid. While this book began as a work project, it took on aspects of the sacred as we heard persons tell their stories. We sat in the home of one husband and wife for five hours while they talked. Before we left they thanked us for listening to their experiences about the husband's continuing recovery from addiction. Their thorough recounting had helped them explore and synthesize parts of their lives in a new way.

This couple eventually decided not to include their story in this collection, which reminds us that healing and caring is slow and persistent work, and, in that way, out of touch with much that characterizes our present world.

Shared Burdens deals not only with those wonderful moments when the church functioned smoothly as soother of hurts, cleanser of wounds, and ointment for healing, but also recognizes times when the church failed, or even contributed to the pain of its members. People stumbled, didn't always know whether to offer love if they couldn't sanction the victim's behavior, prolonged dependency at times, and missed plenty of occasions to do good.

We are most grateful to the people who shared their experiences with us. As we've indicated, not all of the stories we heard are printed here. Some remain too painful, too unresolved. Recognizing those situations and more, we offer these stories for their inspiration and encouragement, so that mutual aid and the sharing and bearing of each other's burdens will continue.

—*Glen A. Roth*
—*Sue V. Schlabach*

A Community
Responds

During my six weeks in the hospital for a bone marrow transplant, God came to me through many of my brothers and sisters from Park View Mennonite Church.

Some came and stayed by my bedside for several hours even though I could barely talk or was not alert. Others sang to me from the hymnal. Some people brought pictures of their summer vacations and walked me through their experiences. I was lent books, cassette and video tapes, and given all kinds of gifts: raspberry iced tea and cheeseburgers, homemade soups and breads, freshly made applesauce, and frozen yogurt. Many people prayed with me. Our Sunday school class sponsored a benefit dinner to help with expenses.

When I came home we were given meals; people volunteered to come clean the house. Friends came to help with the laundry, can peaches and applesauce, stow strawberry jam and blueberries in our freezer, take care of the children, and share gifts of money with us. While cleaning our house someone discovered our vacuum cleaner to be virtually powerless so they replaced it. I could see that all these people were instruments of God in our lives.

Jan Glanzer
Harrisonburg, Virginia

Blessed Trinity

Leon and Audrey Roth Kraybill have a unique family. They share here about the moment when they learned how their lives would be changed, and the way their church and community helped them cope with the sudden adjustments.

Leon: When we sat in the waiting room until our turn for the ultrasound, we were ordinary people, just part of the crowd. Audrey was in her twenty-first week of pregnancy and was exceptionally large. The possibility that we might have twins was the most overwhelming option we could think of.

When Audrey got up on the table with the ultrasound device on her abdomen, the technician almost immediately said, "There's a reason why you're big. There are two in there." But we looked at each other in disbelief when the technician gasped and said, "And there is a third one." I could feel the blood rush to my head, and my first instinct was to tell her to turn off the machine. I was afraid she would find more.

Audrey: I felt the sensation of being pulled into a wind tunnel. I couldn't get air. Leon came over to me and our tears mingled. We just held each other and tried to put the news in perspective. I remember, too, a feeling of loss—that our family was probably, at this moment, finished and it had hardly begun. The one pregnancy took care of everything!

Yet the results of the ultrasound showed each baby to be healthy, on schedule with backbones and hearts, all emptying their bladders. That day Leon and I became very stubborn together. We had these children now, and we were going to fight and do everything we could to keep them. On the ultrasound screen I saw a little hand go by and a face. I told Leon it looked like Jacob, our two-year-old son. They weren't so foreign then. They weren't fetus A, B, and C, as the technician called them. They were our children.

Leon: These were the first triplets ever at that facility. When we were finished the technicians were grinning from ear to ear. We were devastated and scared. When we went back to the waiting room everyone clapped for us. The realization hit us that our life was permanently changed. We were going to be on display. We made the transition from being ordinary people to being parents of triplets. That was not necessarily a happy feeling.

Audrey: I went to a church meeting the next night and was particularly uncomfortable. In the cloak room I told a few of my best friends, and they reacted as I first did, like a blast of air had hit them. We had told Vern and Marilyn Rempel (our pastor couple) already. That night I heard that a rumor was going around the church. Our news had leaked, but most people didn't believe it. So that Sunday we went up front during sharing time. I remember people giving us the look of "What's so important you have to stand in front?"

Leon: My standard line of introducing it by then was: we found out this week that we're not having just one baby.

Audrey: After he said that I saw nice smiles in the congregation. Then he said, with a sort of choked voice, "We're having more than two; we're having triplets." Those smiles dissolved to fear, pity, and a lot of concern. At that point people wiped their noses and there were sniffles. We were pretty choked up, too.

We shared that it would be a high risk pregnancy, we didn't know what the future would be, and that we were scared. We just asked for prayer. Afterwards people hugged us and really committed their prayer support.

At 22 weeks of pregnancy (normal pregnancies go 40 weeks) I looked like a full-term, overdue, very miserable pregnant woman.

Leon: The average triplet pregnancy is 33 weeks. We knew if we could make it through 30 weeks there would be a chance of things going well. We also had to coordinate our lives. We would need a larger vehicle, our house would be too small for three additional people, and how would our two-year-old son, Jacob, deal with three new personalities?

A week after the ultrasound, Audrey was put on bed rest and over the next month and a half became less and less active. Jacob needed to be with relatives during the day because Audrey was unable to keep up with him.

Audrey: At 29 weeks I went in for a routine check-up. It turned out my cervix was already six to ten centimeters dilated. My doctor sent me straight to the hospital and made plans for a cesarean section delivery. I called Leon.

Leon: The anesthesiologist threw me scrub pants as I walked through the door. Just when they were going to roll Audrey in, the obstetrician (in retrospect it seems divine) said, "Maybe we can hold this off a little bit. Let's try to stop it with medication." The medicine slowed down the labor, but it seemed touch and go.

It became a waiting game. I was working full-time, then coming home to get Jacob, and going in to visit Audrey.

At that point we felt people gathering around us. People from church brought meals twice a week, and our families contributed the other meals. Lots of cards arrived, and people came to visit Audrey.

Her medicine was so strong that her vision was impaired, and she could hardly read. She began hallucinating, having strange visions of pressed salmon cakes and sumo wrestlers. She'd tell the nurse and me, and we could hardly keep from laughing. But, behind all that was the fear of losing the babies. We were fighting for every one even though we knew the task would be overwhelming. Audrey managed to hold off the delivery for three and a half additional weeks.

Audrey: Leon got walking pneumonia during the time I was hospitalized. I was concerned for him and was under complete stress. My mind was fried from the medicine, which caused severe reactions. Even a normal voice sounded like a shout. I had my room temperature turned down to the fifties, and still it felt like Tabasco sauce was flowing through my veins. I was aware, but felt like an elderly person who can't remember that she just tied her shoes. Every ounce of my strength was poured into getting those three babies here. Nothing was left over. I wanted desperately to give Jacob attention, but physically I was in excruciating pain, and when he would touch me, it would reverberate through my entire body.

It was an incredible experience. Although I couldn't have many visitors in my fragile physical and mental state, I had this image of people right there holding us, even though they weren't physically present. Somehow we were upheld by that image. It was a kind of tangible presence. It was one of the times I've never had a doubt of God's presence. There were moments when I would cry out, "God, I just can't do this anymore!" and a card would come saying, "I'm praying for you." It was the most difficult part of my life, but God was very real to me. Since then I've felt that to tell someone "I'm praying for you" is an incredible gift—more powerful than we know.

At 32½ weeks I rolled over in bed and my water broke. Each night before I went to bed I took a pain pill so I could sleep, but that night I hadn't. If I had taken medication I wouldn't have been lucid enough to call Leon.

Leon: She called and very matter-of-factly said, "We're going to have some babies."

Audrey: There was a Mennonite nurse on duty that night who said a prayer with Leon and me before we went into the operating room. Later I found out that a woman who heard about us and had written to us regularly throughout my pregnancy woke up that night about the time when my water broke. She couldn't sleep so she thought of us and prayed for the babies. I had a real peace and knew that whatever happened would be okay.

The doctors were hyper. I told my obstetrician I wanted spinal anesthesia so I could be awake for the delivery. He said if it didn't take effect after two tries he would have to put me under. It failed the first time, but worked the second. I was so thankful.

Leon: It takes two or three minutes to get into the uterus by way of cesarean section. The babies were born one minute apart: 2:30, 2:31, and 2:32 a.m. Three girls. We went to the Intensive Care Unit after the recovery room and looked at each one in turn.

Audrey: We were so exhausted and relieved, there was not a lot of time to bond. We just wanted to sleep.

I gained a lot of compassion in the hospital for people who are hospitalized long-term. Leon's life was so hectic I didn't get a toothbrush for a week, and a friend finally brought me deodorant. I felt like I had complete lack of control and was totally cut off from the world.

Coming home in the car was like an amusement park ride. I was floating; the breeze on my face felt like silk after being isolated for so long.

Leon: The girls came home within a month. We put up a sign outside the door for each baby as, one by one, we brought them home. A neighbor down the street thought we had one baby and couldn't decide on a name. Each new baby came home while Jacob was sleeping, and after awhile we joked that he was probably afraid to go to sleep, because every time he awoke there was a new baby.

In the first six months the amazing thing in the community was the tremendous support we received. Our church brought us meals for three months. People seemed to come out of the woodwork—people we didn't know, but who were uncles, cousins, friends of people we knew. In that first half year there were only three nights when we were by ourselves. All the other nights at least two people came and slept there and took care of the children so we could sleep.

Even though we were exhausted, we didn't necessarily feel rested in the morning. But for 24 hours a day we had two- to four-hour shifts of two persons helping us. We calculated that over 3,000 volunteer hours were given in those first six months. We saw people from a new side, the human compassion side.

Audrey: I learned to receive the blessing of allowing people to give, and the joy of receiving. I was taught, like many Mennonite women, to give, give, give. So the lesson for me was to allow people to give as a way of allowing God to bless them.

We saw reunions in our living room when shifts overlapped—people who hadn't seen each other since their dating years in the Fifties. Two sisters came once a week, and we followed them through the decline of their father's health and then his funeral. The woman who prayed for us the night of the delivery came faithfully twice a week, and another family came each Monday night until we didn't need full-time help anymore. It was a real tangible support network.

There were exhausting aspects of having people in our house 24 hours a day. At first I felt like I should serve them food, but there was no way to entertain people all the time. I learned I didn't have to. I had conflicting feelings of wanting to be a gracious host and knowing we didn't have the energy.

There was a lack of privacy, like we were living with two roommates all the time. And that fishbowl feeling at home paralleled the feeling that our lives had become a fishbowl by having the triplets. People weren't invasive, but how much can you take? There was always someone in our living room, kitchen, bathroom. I remember going around the corner into the kitchen and just crying my heart out, but I didn't want anyone to see me. I just didn't feel like explaining or talking. Each day I would go to the door in the morning to answer the doorbell. Sometimes I didn't know the people on the other side. It was like a circus with no humor. Then there were the regulars we knew were coming, and that was always a relief.

I felt like everyone in Lancaster County is going to know that I didn't wash my floor today, or everyone will know I yelled at Jacob. One time I yelled at Jacob and expected someone to say, "That's awful." Instead, the woman on duty said, "It must be hard to parent in front of people under such stress." Those kinds of moments reinforced the sense that people were saying, "We are all human and all sharing this journey. We're with you."

We felt so overwhelmed with love and support. It's given me a deep commitment to others in need. As I see need, and as I can, I want to be there. I hope this is a lesson I never lose. It made a profound impression on me.

Leon: Pervasive for me has been the loss of control. Loss for Audrey, being unable to do things for herself in the hospital. The sense of other people taking care of our children because we are unable to do it ourselves. The sense of being full-time in child care. There is little time to nurture myself or our marriage relationship, to take care of the house or spend the time I'd like to with Jacob. Right now we're family-focused and have to put our energy into that. But there is a loss of time to play and sit with each other. When we do sit together, we don't have the energy to talk. There's also the loss of church involvement. We dropped out of our small group and can't be as active in the church as we were before.

Audrey: An underlying theme for me is grieving. Most people who look at our situation don't see grief as being part of it, but it is profoundly so for me. We've grieved the lack of one-on-one time that we will never be able to give to our children or each other. This experience has pushed me quickly and dramatically into major adulthood, which I resisted at first. I don't get a chance to grow into parenthood, one child at a time, and learn from my mistakes.

Now I'm finding the grief is beginning to heal and that gratefulness is filling its place. I am grateful for our children, and I know that our family will have many good times together. If I would not have allowed that grieving, I wouldn't be able to celebrate. Everyone has a time in life when they face their mortality and the limitations life has put on them. I feel like I'm coming through now with more faith and hope. But it doesn't always feel that way. It's pretty scary sometimes.

Leon: After six months we needed more personal space and were more ready to have less volunteer help. We have a full-time person here during the day and volunteers three evenings a week. More and more we're doing it ourselves. When all the kids are in a good mood it goes well. Other times it gets hectic. We still need the help of others for our emotional health.

Audrey: I've found mutuality to be like a chain. You pass it on. As I hold on to one hand I keep my other hand open. I said to someone, "How can I give it all back?" and they said, "You can't. You just pass it to the next person."

It was a June day and from the west end of our hayfield I saw flames high in the air. I had prayed for help to decide the best possible use of the old barn, and now it was going up in smoke. I thought, "God doesn't want us to be dairy farmers." Then I looked at our yard full of friends, neighbors, and a few strangers and wondered where all of the people came from so fast.

One woman said, "If God wants you to milk cows, he'll build a barn for you."

"Are you nuts?" I thought.

However, after a meeting that Sunday at Strawberry Lake Mennonite Church where we attend, I went away feeling like God would really do it for us. Although at the time I could not see how, it was done in phases, one step at a time. There were times when I was depressed or discouraged and ready to throw in the towel. But someone always came up with the words I needed. Now I know that help came from God through many different people.

One day the next March, a major step began. Once again our yard filled with people, making a joint effort to put up a new structure. The following October the youth used the new hayloft for a community party. How fitting since they all helped to build it! Then in December we sent the first milk on a truck to market. The time between the fire and that first delivery felt both long and short. I know if it had come easily, I probably wouldn't appreciate it nearly as much as I do now.

We thank God and all of the people he brought to our aid. The members of our church and community provided us with financial physical, spiritual, and emotional help when we needed it. They even provided us with food for strength to keep working. I'm here to say that the lady was not nuts. God does build barns.

Archie and Rebel Stiyer
Ogema, Minnesota

GROWING FROM GRIEF

Naomi Moyer will never forget even the most ordinary moments from that particular July 16. It was a hot summer day in the mountains of central Vermont where Naomi and her husband Steve live. Many of Steve's family members reside nearby, and that week his brother's family was visiting from Virginia. They planned daily gatherings to swim at the reservoir lake where Steve's parents live. On his way to work, Steve took their six-year-old son, Sam, to the lake to spend the day with his cousins. Naomi had errands to do and took 3-year-old Ada with her. She and Ada planned to join the others at the lake in the afternoon.

"On the way home from our shopping trip, I stopped at the lake to pick up Sam," says Naomi. "I told him we would come back later to swim, but my sister-in-law, Ann, offered to watch Sam and Ada if they wanted to stay. I kissed Ada on the head and watched her drag a plastic zebra float down to the water.

"As I drove home I thought I should call over there to make sure Ada was wearing her inflatable Swimmies on her arms. I had just gotten in the door and was putting some groceries away when the phone rang. It was Steve's brother, Brad, so I told him to see that Ada had the Swimmies on. I felt an urgency about it, but he mustn't have noted that tone in my voice.

"I finished putting the food away and was going to start supper before going down to the lake. Then the phone rang a second time and I knew something was wrong. This time it was Ann asking me whether Ada was with me. 'No,' I said, 'she's with you.' 'No, we looked all around,' Ann said. 'We can't find her.'"

Naomi rushed down to her in-laws home, the whole time repeating out loud, "Please protect her!" When she arrived, Ada was still missing. A man who was swimming nearby had joined in the search and, when he dived where Naomi pointed, he surfaced with Ada in his arms. She had been under the water for about 20 minutes.

Naomi and Ann began CPR immediately, but saw that Ada's pupils were dilated and knew she had drowned. Sam and his cousins were gathered around them.

"Is this too hard on the kids?" Naomi thought, but realized, "No, Sam will have to understand that Ada is gone and what it means when people die." She herself let out raw and primal cries, like ones she has since heard from mothers giving birth in the maternity ward where she is a nurse. "I think both birth and death are times of letting go. And at that moment I began that letting go."

Naomi and Steve moved through the following days, numb with grief and sleeplessness. Several people from Bethany Mennonite Church, where Naomi and Steve are members, took leadership in arranging meals for the Moyers. Others offered lodging for relatives who would be arriving. In addition, one church friend acted on his knowledge that Steve and Naomi weren't financially equipped to handle funeral and burial expenses. He arranged for the funeral home to send all bills to him, and the church agreed to pay them.

"There were people in the church and in the community that inundated us with food," Naomi remembers. "I was amazed by how people-rich we were. We got a lot of cards. Many were from people that had also lost children, and I realized how connected we were to other people. We witnessed the compassionate human spirit. Though I could never pay people back, I hoped I could learn from this experience to be more compassionate and share what I have with others."

Naomi found her faith to be essential in the days that followed. Many decisions had to be made, but all she could focus on was Ada's memorial service. "It has to be hopeful," she thought. She couldn't bear to think it wasn't.

The day before the funeral, Steve and Naomi brought Ada home. Church friends made the arrangements for people to gather there for the viewing. The atmosphere resembled a picnic, Naomi recalls. Friends and relatives stayed into the evening hours that day and the next after Ada's burial, sitting on lawn chairs around the garden overlooking the ridges below the house. Steve and Naomi found it helpful to be encircled by people. Details were taken care of by the church. "It was a very hot day and they made sure everyone had something cold to drink and food to eat. I didn't worry about anything. I let people be in charge and that was helpful to them. Afterwards someone said, 'It was so nice you let us minister to you.' I remember thinking, 'I can't imagine going through this without a group of people who care very deeply about me.'"

Part of dealing with Ada's death included forgiveness. Naomi and Steve had to explore a gamut of emotions before they could forgive Ann, their sister-in-law who volunteered to watch Ada at the time she drowned. In doing so, they invited Ann into the process. Ann, a Mennonite pastor in San Diego, suffered with her own grief and guilt, and the three stayed in regular contact—Ann encouraging them to feel the anger and disappointment they had toward her, and Steve and Naomi offering Ann the grace of their continued forgiveness.

"The only way I could heal was through a greater understanding of forgiveness and God's grace," Naomi says. "I had to forgive the human part of us, because it was an act of human error that caused Ada's death. Part of our humanness is that we are unwhole, but not in a bad way. We are greatly in need of God. That became evident to me and was actually comforting. Ann's relationship with me was too important to throw away. But I couldn't honestly forgive Ann, and continue to forgive her, without feeling the whole range of emotions. I had to let a higher power know just how horrible I felt.

"Forgiveness is a daily ongoing thing. It doesn't mean that every day I have to forgive Ann; it's more that I've chosen to love her. Not forgiving Ann would deface Ada, and I know Ada loves Ann. For us, forgiving is not saying, 'It's okay.' Forgiving is saying we have chosen to live and we want Ann to live too."

Naomi was very touched by the emotions shown by people at their church. Ada was the first person who died while regularly attending Bethany, and the tragedy of the event was new territory for its members. "I didn't realize to what extent a little person could affect so many people," says Naomi. "It was comforting to know they hurt with us. One man wrote us a letter and said, 'This has been a loss, and though not as shattering for us as for you, it is a loss, for the church. We expected this little girl to come bouncing in every Sunday.'

"The church was helpful in showing me that the Bible can help us in suffering. I could relate to the anguishes of David. 'The Lord is nearer to the broken-hearted and saves the crushed in spirit,' Psalm 34:18. Those were the things that sustained me."

Though Naomi and Steve felt very cared for by the church, they did not always feel that people understood the emotions of their grief, or the longevity of it. Two months after Ada's death, Naomi and Steve were asked to do a morning worship service about their experience and grief issues. Naomi and Steve agreed, aware that the church was also suffering.

"If we were asked to do a service now, we would do it much differently, offering ways to help people and even facilitate their grieving. But at that time neither of us felt we could even scratch the surface. We did what we could do best, which was to tell our story. There wasn't a lot that I could give to people. I was depleted in every respect—emotionally, spiritually, and physically. At that time I didn't doubt God's existence, but I didn't like him. There was nothing pleasurable about heaven, and I even questioned whether there was one. I was totally depleted. It was all I could do to take care of myself, Steve, and Sam. I spent most of the time crying. Before Ada died I wasn't the type that cried a lot. I was a very easygoing, happy person. To think that I might be this way for the rest of my life was pretty overwhelming.

"In nearly every entry in my journal, I wrote that I was exhausted. Physical exhaustion is normal for a grieving person. I read books on what to expect, physically, emotionally, and spiritually when I was grieving, and followed their advice. But I wish the church had been more educated about grieving in order to offer me those things.

"The pastor from the local Congregational church gave me some concrete ideas of how to deal with day-to-day living. She told me to specifically make sure that I took care of myself, that we as a couple took care of each other, and met Sam's needs. She recommended we spend at least one night a week alone with each other and that each of us have quiet time alone. I found real specific things to be helpful in the early months because so much of our reality had been blown away."

Throughout the healing process, Naomi's image of God changed. She needed to examine and rethink who God was, while searching for evidence of heaven. "As Christians, we believe that death is not the end, but we don't act like it. I was gripped with sadness and needed to hear that there was something hopeful and positive for Ada after death. Sometimes people just said I was morbid because I talked about death. That was hard because I needed to talk about it and have people acknowledge that my grieving wasn't over.

"I believe God cried tremendously when Ada was drowning. I think he said, 'Oh no, I put this law in place and this little girl is going to drown. But I will be with you.' I can't imagine going through this not having the sense that someone larger cared about me. Jesus was a part of God, and children are a part of us and God. I thought about God grieving over Jesus and Ada. God's grace covered me and he said, 'I do know what it feels like to have a child die.' It was comforting to know that God was familiar with my pain.

"The nursing staff I work with really ministered to me. I was fortunate because they knew what grief was like—either from personal experience, or from watching people go through it, and also from being educated in it. For the first year I was given every holiday off from work, which was important because I had to face the fact that Ada wasn't at this holiday, like she was at the last one. My employers made sure that I never got too tired. I think that is why I didn't get sick. They knew that grief was physically demanding.

"Through the long haul of it I talked with two dear nursing friends at work who understood my needs. In addition I had a church friend with whom I could share. Each would call on a weekly basis or visit me and let me talk, which is what I needed. I had to work out my anger and find appropriate ways to do that. The church did not encourage me to vent my anger. Probably the biggest gift my friends gave me was to allow me to vent my anger for as long as I needed to.

"It is important that I let other people know this experience in my life. I'm not doing anyone any service by carrying this pain by myself. It is not helpful to myself or others if I don't share it. One of my friends had her own grief to deal with that October when her mother died of cancer. Since then I have been able to minister to her, which was nice after I allowed her to help me through my suffering."

"Grief was my close companion for a whole year. With everything I did I thought, 'This is the first time I've done this without Ada.' I went to a wedding and I had to think that Ada would never grow up and get married. I went to a baby shower and thought, 'My little girl will never have children and I will never be a grandmother to her kids.' There was a first for everything.

"Now grief just comes to visit. It will always be a part of me. I would hate to think otherwise. I don't know how our souls are connected with our children, but a part of my self died when Ada died."

Almost two years after Ada drowned, Naomi recognizes that her life is changed, and changed permanently. "I will have to learn to live with the knowledge that kids drown and be able to go swimming anyway. I remember diving into the water last summer and being very aware of its powers. I wish I could erase it. I took Sam down to the lake and I couldn't read a book. I had to sit and watch him. Swimming will be forever altered. Huckleberry Finn said when he was young he remembered seeing the mauve sky and thinking it looked so pretty, but when he grew up he knew that a sky like that meant a nasty storm was coming. You just view life a little differently and you can't erase that. The innocence is gone."

I was a new pastor at the Des Moines Mennonite Church in Iowa when I heard a promoter of refugee sponsorship say, "If you sponsor refugees you will come to love them." We were soon given opportunity to test the statement.

Shortly thereafter, the former pastor called me from Washington, Iowa. Two families in his church had sponsored the Ha and La Baccam family from Thailand. Now the Baccams were moving to Des Moines for Ha's further language training and work in the printing trade. The pastor asked if I would invite them to the church. He also contacted Doyle and Ilene Miller about helping the Baccams. Ilene soon found La a housekeeping job at the Lutheran Hospital.

Doyle became chairman of the developing Resettlement Committee. At Ha's request a house was rented for their family, and soon they were sponsored by our congregation. Later the church purchased a house when we sponsored more members of La's extended family.

New arrivals and other former refugees who settled in Des Moines joined in attendance at our church. At Des Moines Mennonite Church they found a gathering of people who shared their language, homeland memories, and experiences of being assisted in surviving in the United States.

Ha Baccam became a caring lay leader, then a licensed minister, and eventually an ordained minister and scripture translator for the growing community of Thaidam, Lao, and Vietnamese refugees who were sponsored by Mennonites in Iowa and Nebraska. It is true—members of our congregation love and embrace these people who have become a part of our church family.

Paul H. Martin
Des Moines, Iowa

A Presence
As Thick As Mud

Loren Todd was, at age 18, a recent high school graduate and a vital member of the work force on his family's farm.

It was a cold, wet Monday morning in early April. A customer had come to buy roasted soybeans, so we went to the barn on my uncle's neighboring farm to load the beans. In the process of loading the beans, the end of the auger lifted up. When I instinctively put my hand on a gear box to push it down, my loose-fitting coat sleeve caught a shear bolt on the rapidly moving shaft, and it took me for a ride.

Time seemed to stop. All the clothing from my waist up was ripped off and wrapped around my right arm, holding me to the spinning shaft. Somehow the machine pulled my head in against the shaft, protecting it, but beating the rest of my body against the floor. The first thing that went through my mind was, "I'm going to die," and I thought of my parents and friends. My thought process seemed very slow because my body was moving so rapidly. My feet and left arm were hitting the floor about three times every second, and we estimated that I was in motion for six seconds.

My father was nearby on another tractor, but by the time he reacted to turn off the auger, the damage was done. The gear box split in half and I fell to the floor, laid out on my back with all my limbs perfectly in line. When I opened my eyes I was surprised to still be in the barn. I saw my broken and discolored left arm lying beside me, and I knew it was beyond repair. Though I felt no pain, my left arm was almost severed.

Meanwhile my father was cutting my clothing away to release my right arm from the shaft. The whole time he was hysterical, while I somehow remained calm.

My aunt came out to the barn, but my dad would not let her come in. I talked to her through the doors of the shed and told her to pray for my legs. From the waist down I was paralyzed, and the rest of my body was numb from shock. I felt as though I should be able to get up and walk away, but I was not able to move. The only thing I felt was the cold seeping in underneath the jacket my father had thrown over me. I kept telling him to relax, but he was still in hysterics when he left to call the ambulance.

The whole time I remained conscious and calm, knowing that I was going to live. I figured if I had survived this far, I wouldn't die now! Since my body was in shock there was no profuse bleeding from where I had lost my arm. In fact, I bled more from inch-long cuts on my head and my heel than anywhere else.

The fire company arrived first. I had been talking nonstop, and suddenly became short of breath from a collapsed lung. They gave me oxygen, and then soon the ambulance workers were all around me.

In the ambulance I began to slip in and out of consciousness. I remember being slapped to stay awake. It didn't seem very long before they were wheeling me into Lancaster General Hospital's Emergency Room. They put me on a table and went right to work. When we got to the hospital I asked, "I'm going to lose my arm, right?" They didn't hesitate in saying yes, and I said, "Okay, let's forget about that and start healing the rest of me."

I'll never forget how I reacted to the guy who was going to stitch the cut on the back of my head. When you go in the Emergency Room they just take a shaver and zap... shave away sloppily. I said, "Don't shave a spot on my head!" Here I lay with a broken body and I was worried about my hair! I had just gotten my hair cut and a perm in back. He was nice enough to trim just the area around the cut!

Then the shock wore away and I began to feel pain in my upper body. I begged to be put under, and, although my time on that table was only 45 minutes, it seemed to last for hours. They put a tube in my chest for breathing and prepared me for emergency surgery to reconstruct my right knee and remove my left arm.

They allowed my parents and pastor, Carl Steffy, to see me before surgery. I was pleased to see how calm they were, especially my mom. I expected her to respond as my father had. I am grateful that I was conscious during that time to assure them that I would be okay.

I spent 10 terrible days in the Trauma Unit. On the Sunday after my arrival I had a six and a half hour back operation. The outcome would determine whether or not I would ever walk again. I had already started to have some feeling in my lower body, so it was clear to the doctors that my spinal cord wasn't severed. In surgery they repaired nerve damage and put steel rods in the two sections where my back was broken.

The back operation was a success. Afterward I was put on a tilting bed that rocked back and forth to prevent me from getting pneumonia. I had broken seven ribs (five on one side; two on the other), and every time I'd rock to one side I felt excruciating pain. Daily, I was pricked up and down my legs to see if I could detect any feeling returning. At first the sensation was spotty and inconsistent, but today there is only one spot on my right thigh where I don't have feeling.

Each time I grew a little stronger I'd go back in for surgery. My third and last operation was to repair shredded muscles in my right arm and damaged ligaments in my left knee. Then I began my recovery.

In the Trauma Unit, I was heavily sedated, and it seemed to me that I didn't sleep for those 10 days. I would doze, but I was awakened every hour around the clock. Also, I didn't eat anything other than one dish of green jello during those first 10 days. My weight dropped 70 pounds, from 205 to 135, in the first two weeks of my stay. I don't think I have eaten green jello since!

Fortunately I was allowed to have visitors. My friends had to keep walking around the room because I kept tilting on that bed, but I was thankful they were allowed to come see me. My friends upheld me. They were the ones who told me, "If anyone can make it, you can. You are strong-willed, Loren." I had never noticed that in myself before, but they had seen it.

It was through my church that a lot of people found out about the accident and began praying for me. Within a day, people knew in Oregon (where friends of mine go to school), Florida, and other parts of the United States. The Mennonite chain stretches far, and it works.

Even when I was alone, I could feel the outpouring of prayer and support. It was a physical presence as thick as mud that I could feel in the room with me.

Two days before I celebrated my nineteenth birthday, I moved from Trauma into a room of my own. I count that day the greatest in my life, even in light of my dire circumstances. I had an especially difficult time sleeping the night before, because I knew something special was planned.

My friends had arranged a party with cake and punch in the waiting room, and my parents brought an enormous basket overflowing with several hundred cards from friends and people at church.

Because of my high fever, only two people could be in the room at any one time, so I didn't get too hot. Mom kidded me that I was going through menopause because I also had heat flashes. I sweated profusely, and my bed got soaked and had to be changed twice a day. When people weren't coming in, friends would put an ice-cold washcloth on my forehead and read cards to me.

That whole day I was so excited to see everyone. It was a very emotional day for me because the evidence of how much these people cared for me was overwhelming. They kept coming right up until 8:30 p.m. when visitor hours ended. I was dead tired, and slept through the night.

That day marked the beginning of a new life for me. I was in the hospital, the worst place to be, but I was having the greatest day of my life. I think God had a hand in making it so good, giving me the kick in the rear I needed to be motivated for all of the physical therapy that lay ahead.

I sometimes felt swamped during those early days, because 20 to 25 people came to see me every day. Sometimes I was overwhelmed and needed a break. It was great to see them, but I was also glad for time alone. Later, when I moved to the fourth floor and began therapy, the visitors slacked off, and I had my solitude then. I made friends in the hospital too, nurses and other personnel. I went out of my way to get to know people, and most of the hospital knew who I was. Three or four friends came daily to see me, which was more manageable than before.

I was completely helpless for six weeks. All I could move was my head. I had to be fed, and I couldn't get a drink, scratch an itch, or move from my bed without assistance. I was at ground zero physically.

During this time several psychologists told me I would experience severe depression and prepared me to deal with it. I told them it wouldn't happen to me. I had a 100% positive attitude. I was told from the start that I might not walk again, but was convinced I would. I told myself I was going to walk and do most of the things I did before. The forecasted depression never came.

They first began therapy on my right arm, which was very stiff. That was mildly painful, but tolerable. My legs were going to be the therapy challenge. The first time I saw my legs was when they took the casts off. They looked like toothpicks, with my knees larger than my thighs. I was always active in soccer, volleyball, and softball. I did it all. Seeing my legs looking so malnourished was difficult. My casts, too, had been a security, and leaving them behind left me feeling vulnerable. I wore braces after their removal.

Once I regained movement in my right arm, I gained new freedoms, like the ability to feed myself. I no longer had to wait and watch my food get cold until someone came to feed me. I was finally able to use a wheelchair. For seven and a half weeks I hadn't seen anything outside a hospital room, and now I was permitted to go outside when friends visited. Some friends even came on Friday and Saturday nights, which I thought was unheard of. They told me going out wasn't the same without me along. I'd hop in my wheelchair and we'd go outside. I had come into the hospital when the weather was cold, but began moving outside on beautiful spring days.

The pain was nearly unbearable when I started therapy for my legs. In spite of the pain, I enjoyed physical therapy. I started going for a few hours a day, and for the first three weeks I sat in a whirlpool to help heal my infected leg. As I improved, the hours of therapy increased, and eventually I was in therapy for a full day. At first we had to convince my knees that they could bend, and we started muscle stimulation to get my muscles to contract and build because they had deteriorated to practically nothing. Then we moved to weights, and I was fitted for a prosthetic arm.

Toward the end of July I stood for the first time. It took about five people to get me up, because I needed support under my arms. In effect, I was trying to hold myself up more with my arms instead of using my legs to do the work. I felt extremely tall, because when you're at wheelchair level all the time you're always looking up.

I practiced standing, then started walking between parallel bars. Finally I was able to use a walker with a crutch under my arm to support myself. I gradually did more and more learning to walk without assistance from others. By the time I got out in August, I was walking with only a crutch.

I couldn't walk very far at first. I had to be extremely careful because I couldn't lift my legs right, and I fell easily. In fact, I fell many times, but wasn't hurt seriously. I wore a back brace to protect my back. When I fell, I'd turn and catch myself on the brace.

Four years have passed since my accident. Walking feels fairly normal now, except for my limp. I'm not as far along as I'd like to be, and progress is slower than I had hoped. But walking is the best therapy, they tell me, and I try to keep active. I don't have the movement I should in the ankle that was broken, and that makes it hard to lift my toes. This is because my right leg is still weak. I am currently talking with my doctor about possible surgery options.

Looking back, I see my progress. I got rid of my cane a year after the accident. I threw my back brace away after two months. I was told to wear it for a year. I was told to keep wearing my leg braces, but I threw them away after a year. I took one off first, and saw that my leg was getting stronger without it, so I decided if it was going to impede my progress I didn't want it. It was a risk I was willing to take. Now, however, there are more months between the milestones.

I work for Premier Communications, Inc. and on my family's farm part-time. I can't get away from farming. I work around machines all the time, but I'm much more cautious now. The machine that injured me no longer works, but I use one like it. Safety devices have sprung up all over our farm. If I have another career, farming will have to connect with it somehow because it is such a deep part of me.

I have never grieved the loss of my arm. I knew if I could walk again, I'd get along without it. I have been able to use my experience to help other people in similar situations. I spoke about prosthetics to an Amish man who had lost his arm in a harvester. He could see my attitude about losing an arm, and I know it helped him. I think the way I act and carry myself says something to people. They see that I am not that conscious of my disability. People notice my limp more than the missing arm, which proves that my prosthetics people are doing their job!

Without the church and supportive friends I couldn't have made it through the suffering so smoothly. I was in the hospital for four and a half months, and my pastor, Carl Steffy, visited me almost every day. He always shared a Bible verse, and it was ironic how it usually fit my need for that particular day. It was almost humorous how it worked out.

I have learned to value life so much more than I did previously. I value my family, friendships, nature. Even though my hospital experience was long and, in some ways, bad, I made a lot of friends, and I value that highly. I rarely go through a day without aches and pains, but I've learned to deal with them and am grateful to be alive. A day doesn't pass when I am not thankful to be alive.

Whether it be cleaning yards, cutting wood, washing windows for elderly or sick people, financially assisting with medical bills, or offering transportation, the members of Julesburg Mennonite Church are always there to lend a helping hand. They take food to the ill and give many words of encouragement and prayers. They purchase clothing for those needing clothes.

The church not only shows love to its own, but reaches out to the entire community, helping a family with a sick child whose doctor bills reached far beyond their means, and buying airline tickets for a family who was stranded in Julesburg after a car accident and had no money to return home. Never before have I seen such a caring and sharing church family. I am privileged to be part of this fellowship.

Lois Condy
Julesburg, Colorado

Sightless Insight

Jerri Mast moves confidently through her house, guided by memory and her functioning senses. Her blindness isn't easily apparent. Her blue eyes, prosthetic duplicates of her originals, engage the eyes of anyone she talks with. Jerri lost her sight 10 years ago after recovering from a four-day coma that nearly took her life. The coma was the first sign of kidney failure, which was related to her long-term diabetes.

Jerri and her husband Chester live in Chesapeake, Virginia, a tight-knit rural community where Chester grew up. Many members of their church, Mount Pleasant Mennonite, are also members of their family. The people of this congregation played a large role in helping Jerri and Chester through the stages of illness and subsequent loss.

"I was diagnosed with diabetes when I was six years old," says Jerri, "and lived with it for 25 years with no problems. I regulated my blood sugar, took my insulin shots and watched my diet closely. Even so, a long duration of diabetes will eventually take its toll, and in late 1981 I began to experience a decline in my health."

While on a shopping trip with her family in February a few years ago, Jerri told Chester that she didn't feel well. Chester helped her to the car, and by the time they were home she was comatose. Chester rushed Jerri to the hospital and contacted his father.

Doctors were skeptical that she would live. Their opinion was that Jerri would be in a vegetative state if she survived the coma.

"I have several memories and images from the time I was in the coma. The faces of Chester, our pastor, my parents, and our bishop focused in at different times. At one point I heard our pastor telling me that 1,000 people were praying for me."

"You don't realize how much support is out there until a situation comes up," Chester recalls. "When Jerri was in the

Intensive Care Unit, there was an outpouring of concern and prayer. I can remember being overcome emotionally when I stopped to think about the amount of love we were receiving."

Members of Chester's family took care of the Mast's two children so Chester could stay at the hospital. Letters and cards arrived and a prayer chain went into action. The news spread to other Mennonites across the state of Virginia and to Jerri's home community in Oregon.

To the amazement of her medical team, Jerri survived the coma with little immediate evidence of damage. Instead of a cerebral hemorrhage, which was the original diagnosis, Jerri's coma was an early indicator of kidney failure.

"I recuperated in the hospital for three weeks, and passed the hours between family and church visitors with a favorite pastime, reading. One afternoon, a circle on the page of my book was suddenly gone, replaced by a white circle. 'This is strange,' I thought. 'Maybe I need new glasses.' "

One doctor examined Jerri's eyes and did not discover any abnormalities. However, a retinologist discovered Macula Edema, a fluid retention and swelling in the retina. He then gave her laser treatments to help dry up the fluid. But her retinas did not respond to the treatments and later hemorrhaged, making further laser treatments ineffective. Jerri later had a vitrectomy. This caused glaucoma which, in turn, caused her blindness.

"In June of 1982, our family visited a nearby church to hear a singing group. Afterward the minister asked me if I would consider being anointed. I agreed. Members gathered around me and prayed. I did regain some vision and was able to read from the Bible at the church that night. There was enough improvement that I could read and drive after the anointing. I returned to the retina specialist to have my eyes tested again. 'There's no explanation for this,' he said. We told him that I had been anointed and explained the passage in James 5 that calls for anointing of the sick. He scribbled down the reference. Later when I asked to see my medical records, the specialist had written, 'improved vision due to miracle.'

"My last taste of sight lasted for a month. I soaked in my

surroundings, and often drove short distances in the car. I really believed that my sight was being restored. Then my eyes hemorrhaged again."

Jerri's vision faded gradually and she was able to adjust and learn to live and function with each stage of loss. However, she and Chester clung to the hope that her sight would return. They went to specialists in several East Coast cities, but tests revealed that the damage to her eyes could not be reversed.

Jerri's blindness forced many adjustments within her family. In addition to running his full-time construction business, Chester needed to assume more responsibility for household duties and their two young children, Inga and Shaun.

Living in a rural setting made Jerri feel quite dependent and isolated. Without the option of public transportation, she had to rely on family and friends to drive her to appointments and errands.

"In August of 1983 I had my last light perception. I tried not to be angry with God, but I was very angry at the circumstances. At the same time I felt the presence of God was particularly real, both when I was alone and through the people who spent time with me. People from the church gave us a lot of encouragement, and they also provided financial help with our accumulating medical bills. They were especially helpful with our children, who were nine and three, when I got sick. One woman drove Shaun to preschool and other friends included Inga in activities or drove her to school and church events when Chester couldn't. Their expressions of love to us were a real faith-builder for me. Even though I was hurting over the loss of my eyesight, I felt myself growing spiritually.

"There was a point when I said, 'Lord, I'm going to thank you for this blindness.' I finally felt peace and was able to accept it. After that I contacted agencies for the blind and started learning Braille. I was determined to go on."

A rehabilitation teacher taught Jerri to arrange her kitchen so that she could cook and bake. Another instructor taught her how to use a white cane in unfamiliar settings. Learning Braille and having access to a library of books on cassette tape allowed Jerri to be in touch with literature again. Several years later she went to a rehabilitation center for the blind to brush up on secretarial skills and to learn adaptive Braille equipment.

While still learning to live fully without sight, Jerri developed severe symptoms of kidney failure and needed to undergo dialysis treatments. "Three times a week I would spend three hours having my blood purified. The procedure left me physically exhausted, and by the time I'd recover my energy it was time to go back for another treatment."

Volunteers from the Mount Pleasant congregation helped transport Jerri to her treatments. Meanwhile, family members began to talk about finding a kidney donor so Jerri could have a transplant. Her brother, Duane, matched the medical checkpoints needed for a successful transplant. After praying and agonizing over the issue, Duane felt at peace about giving one of his kidneys to Jerri. He flew to Virginia for the operation. No other members of Jerri's family planned to be present.

"The scheduling of our surgeries coincided with rye-grass harvesting on my parent's farm in Oregon. Dad felt he couldn't leave, but the deacon of my home church arranged for a crew of men and combines to harvest my father's crops. On the day of the transplant surgery, 18 combines arrived at the farm and harvested all 110 acres of rye grass that same day." Ordinarily the harvest would have taken several weeks. Because of this effort, Jerri and Duane's parents were able to be present for the surgeries. Other members of the church community in Oregon remembered them in prayer.

"The transplant took place in Norfolk, Virginia. Duane went into surgery several hours before I did. His kidney was removed and prepped, then transplanted. It started to function before they closed my incision."

Now, eight years after the transplant, Jerri's blood tests are normal and she is less dependent on medication. She has lived without sight for over ten years.

"The helping ministry of the church seems to work best in short-term crisis situations. When you get into extended illness or disability it is difficult for the church to stay tuned in. But there are also many faithful souls in the long haul. I am grateful to have a list of friends who I can call when I need a ride somewhere or when I just need someone to talk to. I tell each of them to say whether it is inconvenient, because I know there is someone else I can ask.

"There are disappointments, too. Occasionally someone offers to take me out for coffee or on a shopping trip, but never follows through. I'd rather they didn't offer. It's hard to know how to deal with that.

"I think some people hesitate to do things with me because they are afraid they will hurt me or run me into something. I try to put them at ease, telling them I need to hold their elbow and that when we come to steps to say 'up' or 'down.' It is a great challenge not to let people over-handicap me."

Though Jerri still relies on Chester and others for many things, she is an avid homemaker and one year was awarded Blind Homemaker of the Year in the state of Virginia. In addition, she has established friendships with other persons who have suffered losses from diabetes. She types weekly correspondence to family and friends in Oregon and considers returning to work as a secretary in the future.

"Last fall I was pleased to be asked to help teach a Sunday school class. I have attended the church regularly, but have not been a teacher or committee member since I lost my sight. It meant a lot to be asked. I help teach first and second grades, telling the children a Bible story each Sunday and assisting the teacher in other ways. The kids have responded very well to me. I was moved by their response when I told them the story of the blind man. The story held more significance for them because I told it to them. Although I don't expect to see in the same way the blind man did, the story also held new power for me."

Although Jerri is blind, she operates with a different kind of vision. She can see the church at work caring for one another in times of need. Of this she is certain. She has been a recipient of this care. And she has responded in kind. For first and second graders at Mount Pleasant Mennonite Church, for example, Jerri has brought a sense of presence and life to the story of the blind man. With her warm and sensitive spirit, she will surely find other ways to help meet needs within the congregation.

A severely broken wrist left my husband disabled for nearly six months. We are self-employed, and he needed his wrist for his work. We had recently joined Lower Deer Creek Mennonite Church, and a couple from there, Clarence and Helen Yoder, insisted on helping us.

We raised chickens for the first time that summer, so they organized a chicken-butchering party. For two days in a row, 25 to 35 people came early in the morning with much equipment and joyful hearts of service and quickly butchered 100 chickens for us. They could have done it in one day, but Helen said others would have been disappointed if they couldn't have helped out on the second day! We were deeply impressed with how so many people shared with us during our time of need.

Karma Brokaw
Kalona, Iowa

Disabled By Conflict, United By Fire

The call came over the rural party telephone line, and the word spread throughout the small community in northern Canada: Loewen's barn had burned to the ground.

Normally most of the community congregated before the last blazing timber fell, ready to clean up and prepare for re-building. Instead, the news buzzed across telephone wires and in lowered voices at the local cheese factory and co-op store.

Henry Wiens looked at the whispering groups with disappointment. In the past a barn fire brought the members of this diverse community together. Mennonite, Mennonite Brethren, Holdeman, and Catholic joined in a unique ecumenical fellowship focused on a common task. Fires brought a particular sense of unity. The cleanup and building involved everyone to bring about a visible resurrection in the space of one day. It was ironic how festive these occasions were.

But today Loewen's fire only triggered gossip in the community. Did he have adequate insurance? Was cattle or equipment lost? How did the fire start? These reactions indicated to Henry Wiens that an even greater calamity was brewing in the community. Once the community had moved instinctually to share. Now all action was frozen due to theological conflict among different churches.

Henry drove home past the fields of green grain, bright yellow canola, and blue flax. All of nature was displayed, vibrant and alive, before the backdrop of the snowcapped Rockies, but the human network was dead. Not knowing why, he headed for David Schartner's farm, driven by the feelings that surfaced in him that morning.

He had not been to Schartner's since the conflicts between their churches began. David met him on his way to the house after the morning milking. Yes, he had heard about Loewen's barn, but he continued toward the house, not agreeing to join Henry in a cleanup effort.

"Don't you remember how we always enjoyed organizing things like this before?" Henry asked. "All I want is for you to join me in a barn raising at Loewen's. If we go I believe the others will join us."

David still refused. "We can no longer associate with people with whom we have theological differences. We have to take a stand," he said.

Angry and hurt, Henry blurted out an ultimatum, "I've come to ask you to join me in good work, something I believe Jesus would have us do. I'm going to sit in my car in your driveway as long as it takes for you to join me."

"You can't wait that long," David retorted.

As Henry sat in his car, he regretted his words. And he felt guilty for his method of confrontation. He believed in being flexible and adaptive, and now he felt as though he had violated his own personal convictions. He wondered how long he would have to wait. It was no longer clear to him what Jesus would do.

Inside, David sat at the breakfast table with his family, but found himself unable to pray. He could hear his children rustling around, hungry and puzzled over his long pause.

Henry sank back behind the wheel, thinking of his father. He had always taught him to trust other Mennonites, as well as Jewish and Muslim customers in the store his family owned during his childhood in Russia. Since coming to Canada, Henry vowed to work for the good of family, church, community, and country, having seen in Russia how fragile these things were, and how irretrievable when lost. Now he had made an enemy.

David remained at the table. Anger, fear, defensiveness, and guilt competed for expression within him. In his uncertainty and festering anger, he knew what he had to do. He raised his head to his waiting family and told his oldest son to go start the tractor. They were going to the Loewens to raise a barn.

Henry was too self-absorbed to notice David approaching his car. "Okay, Henry, I'll call my people and we'll be over at Loewens," David said. "But don't think this means we agree theologically!"

Diesel tractors could be heard knocking and sputtering throughout the valley as they converged onto the Loewen property. Men that had whispered in separate groups that morning scooped ashes together, repaired the foundation, and assembled wall studs.

Barely convinced that it was happening, Henry Wiens watched as the blond wood frames were hoisted up and up into the afternoon blue of the heavens. Disaster and loss gave rise to mutuality and celebration involving all ages and both genders.

For the children, the event was hours of undiluted festivity, playing beckon-a-beckon and kick the can. By mid-day the women, had spread tables with an abundance of favorite foods. Everyone gathered around the tables, and children crowded to the front, wide-eyed over such bounty. Hats came off in quiet ritual, and then there was a brief moment of uneasy silence. How would the prayer be offered? Henry Wiens, after a moment of pause, stepped forward and with beaming face said, "Let's sing the song we used to sing in times like this, 'Come we that love the Lord.'" And everyone joined in.

After the feasting, children went back to their play and parents to their work. The act of joining timers and joining voices in song blended as Loewen's new barn continued to rise from the ashes.

This is an adaptation of a true story, told by Jack Dueck. Fictitious names have been used.

My first contact with Mennonites was through agricultural circles. On numerous occasions I witnessed the integrity of Mennonite farmers. One specific incident made a lasting impression on me. I needed to replace the drainage tile on my farm and hired a Mennonite to do the job. When he gave me the estimate, I asked him to write down that the job would not exceed the quoted price. I could not afford to pay more. The man assured me that the bill would not be more than the estimate, but wouldn't put it in writing.

When the work was finished and the bill came, it was actually $4,000 less than the quoted price. Never before had I been given a bill that was less than the estimate. This example of integrity and honesty was a significant factor in my eventual choice to join a Mennonite church.

Michael Greenhough
Kitchener, Ontario

Losing My Husband, My Helper, My Friend

Anna Ruth came home from her part-time job to find her husband, Don, sharpening a saw, with their five children surrounding him, watching and talking. The family planned to attend a Bible study that evening, so she left them in the garage and went to start supper. Don worked as a mason contractor but had taken on a part-time night job when the building trade slowed down. Tonight he intended to go directly to work from the meeting.

While Anna Ruth stirred soup and got plates down from the cupboard, Don came in and suggested, "Let's spend the evening together at home. I just don't like the idea of your coming home from Bible study and putting the children to bed alone."

She slowed down her pace, and the family enjoyed a leisurely meal together. Don thanked her for the delicious meal. He spent time with all the children, playing games and reading stories. When it was time to leave, he mentioned again how good the supper was. He kissed Anna Ruth good-bye, and all the children came running for their kisses. He gave his wife another kiss and was on his way.

A special closeness lingered as they watched him walk to the car and drive away.

Don called me at 10:00 p.m. and said that his foreman came to work late because his daughter had surgery that day. So he decided to stay a while longer and help load trucks. He thought he would be home by midnight. That was fine with me. I would have the coffee ready.

At 12:00 a.m. he called again and said he would not be home until 1:00 or 2:00, and that I had better go to bed. But I said I would wait up.

At 1:20, just as I thought about putting the coffee on, I heard an ambulance siren pierce the still night. The sound laid a heaviness upon me that I couldn't shake. I began to pray, "Lord, bring him home safely." Over and over again I prayed.

I sat on the sofa as if paralyzed by the heaviness. I felt the sensation of a burden tied around me. I sat for nearly three hours, thinking and praying. Maybe he was going to work all night. But I knew he would call. Maybe he thought I went to bed. He would have called anyway. Maybe he was hurt.

Meanwhile, the fire in the wood stove was going out and the house was getting chilly. But I continued to sit. Immobile. Paralyzed.

4:00 o'clock. The house was cold. I hadn't moved from the couch. "God, help me! Help me to accept whatever has happened. Please help me!"

And then, finally, I heard a car. Lights came into the driveway. "Is it our car? No. Is it Don's truck? No." Three car doors slammed instead of one, and the doorbell motivated me to get up. Two state troopers and our pastor met me at the door.

"Is he gone?" I asked. They looked surprised, but moved into the house saying nothing. They led me to the sofa, and we sat down. "Tell me, is he gone?" I asked again.

"Yes. There has been an accident." "Oh, dear God, how can I tell the children?"

Anna Ruth Martin's husband, Donald, was killed in a head-on double fatality automobile collision with a Pennsylvania State policeman at 1:20 a.m., November 5, 1981. She was left with five children, ranging in age from 18 months to 10 years.

The news of Don's death brought painful reality to Anna Ruth's fears. But the long sleepless night helped prepare her for the news that reached her in the early morning hours. Had she been wakened from a deep sleep, the words would have been much more shocking.

Morning came and Anna Ruth's brain was numb. She wondered if she would ever remember things again and be able to plan efficiently. The responsibility for her own life and the lives of her children seemed frightfully heavy.

The burden that had taken hold of her the night before continued to weigh heavily on her chest while she waited for the children to wake up. Only three of her children were old enough to understand what she would have to tell them. One at a time they awoke in sequence of their ages, and she spent time with each one alone, as they expressed their grief.

While she was upstairs comforting the children, the house slowly and quietly filled with family, neighbors, and friends. She came down into rooms full of familiar and loving faces. It was clear that they intended she not bear the pain alone.

When the house emptied and she finally climbed into bed, a feeling of bleakness and aloneness, unlike any she had felt before, consumed her.

That night when I was alone in my room, I felt very naked before God. I was nothing. Gone was my husband, my helper, my friend. Gone was the companionship I had known for 16 years. I was really only half a person who was left to be a parent to five small children. And the half a person that I was couldn't remember, couldn't think ahead, couldn't do anything without extreme effort.

Somehow the emptiness dissipated and God's presence surrounded her, enabling her to sleep peacefully through the night.

For Anna Ruth, losing Don was an uncanny mirror of her father's death. In 1948, when she was almost three, he died in reaction to the wrong medication, leaving her 22-year-old mother to raise three small children. With only an eighth grade education, her mother couldn't do much financially to support her family, so she taught herself to type and set out to get an office job. Although her income was limited, she taught the children that it was possible to be happy without an abundance of material things. Anna Ruth never thought of their family as poor. Her mother's groceries always cost exactly what she had on hand, but there was always enough food on the table.

The circumstances that surrounded Anna Ruth's upbringing enabled her to deal with the immediate stress of single parenting. Her mother proved to be a valuable resource, with many remedies at hand from her own years as a young single mother. Getting the children ready for school in the mornings was no small task, but her mother was there to help her cope. Her mother also scheduled family members to take turns staying overnight with Anna Ruth for four months following the accident, and arranged for someone to be at the house every morning to help dress and feed the children. Anna Ruth never had to concern herself with who came and when. People just arrived. Every night and every morning. For four months.

As each new season began without Don, another list of chores needed to be undertaken. But when the time came, church friends were there to pick apples, work in the garden, mow the lawn, press grapes, sew clothes, and baby-sit. Daily, someone's small gesture lifted a weight from Anna Ruth.

A single mother can easily be abandoned by married friends, but couples went out of their way to include her in events she and Don would have attended together. When the first Valentine's Day arrived, one couple invited her to join them. Neighbors and friends brought a birthday supper to her house and stayed to celebrate with her. Anna Ruth never needed to join a singles support group because her family and friends included her in their activities, just as they had when Don was alive.

Support was there in financial planning as well. A former employee of Don's set up a trust fund for the children, and during the first Christmas season employees from a local bank contributed to the fund instead of having their customary gift exchange.

Paying the bills for Don's business and making out the last payroll checks reinforced the finality of Don's death. She had to deal with other financial matters, and friends stepped in to simplify things for Anna Ruth. A neighbor offered his attorney services free of charge to help her apply for Social Security benefits and take care of other legalities. Support came from school, church, neighborhood, family, and from strangers. Anna Ruth began to realize that gifts of caring and sharing, whether large or small, last a lifetime.

Healing evolved slowly during the coming months and years. At the time of the accident, she felt she would never recover. But Anna Ruth felt God's hand extended to her through the efforts of friends and strangers. But she and her family still faced nagging whys. Don could have driven home another way, like he often did. Why didn't he? He could have talked with the foreman about bear-hunting one minute longer. Why didn't he? In the final analysis, however, the question of "Why?" could not be answered. On numerous occasions after the accident someone would ask her if life got easier as time went on. Her answer was, "No, life in general does not get easier. But God does not promise us an easy life." She has continued to act upon the promise that in all of life God's grace is sufficient.

In some ways the void left by Don's death got bigger with the passing of time. As the children grew older they had a new sense of what it means to be without a daddy. At times they would express self-pity and resentment.

Several years after the accident, my four-year-old daughter became angry when her older siblings talked about Daddy, a daddy she never knew. She wanted to believe that her siblings were making him up, but she gradually came to realize that he was real, and with that came a sense of loss and anger. At times she would say, "It's not fair that other kids have daddies and I don't." During such times she would cry and refuse to be comforted.

Anna Ruth is grateful for the evidence of God shown to her through all that people have done. She hasn't been alone in her journey of pain. Don's memory continues to be an active part of her family's life. In 1988 and 1990 they realized a dream of his by camping on two separate trips across the United States, western Canada, and Alaska.

It was soon after Don died that I came to realize he had left his love with us. When my four-year-old kissed me, she kissed me twice because Daddy couldn't anymore. When I wasn't feeling well, I got all kinds of offers. "Can I rub your back? Should I get you something to drink?" I'll always remember the time I had a

*headache and my three-year-old came, took off my shoes, and
rubbed my feet with hands so small that I could hardly feel them.
From whom did he learn it? Yes, Don's love is still with us.*

Anna Ruth is still busy raising her family and recently saw
her oldest daughter off to college. A large cat lies in the corner
of the kitchen purring. Signs of children fill the
house—drawings, photographs, books. Ten years after the death
of her husband, Anna Ruth Martin has picked up the pieces and
now finds herself shifting from the role of care-receiver to giver.

I have been a member of several churches, but I have never truly experienced caring and sharing as God bids us to do until my husband and I joined the Julesburg Mennonite Church.

My husband had a severe stroke, and with barely adequate income I benefited from lifesaving monetary support and prayer. People from the church came and cut two large trees that I needed for firewood and then sawed, split, and stacked the wood. They raked and mowed the lawn and washed windows to help me prepare for winter.

I came home last week at noon and discovered someone unloading a load of wood from a large pickup truck. He said, "Oh no, I've been caught in the act!" His boots, jeans, and hat showed me that he was Virgil, a friend from church, but perhaps he didn't realize that his angel wings were not invisible and that he was my angel of mercy, making sure I had enough firewood for the winter.

Many other acts of support and assistance go unspoken and remain a quiet mystery because they somehow help us accomplish the impossible. With God all things are possible.

Florence Benner
Julesburg, Colorado

Raising Rafters for Food Aid

The house being built on a residential street in Goshen, Indiana, did not appear unusual to the casual observer. A closer look at the sign in the yard revealed, however, that this house symbolized something quite unique. This house was being built to fight hunger. The workers, straddling roof beams and driving nails, were volunteers, and most of the lumber and building materials, in addition to the land on which the house stood, were donated. And when the house was sold, the $70,000 in proceeds was given to Mennonite Central Committee (MCC) for food relief in drought and famine sites around the world.

The house in Goshen was the birth of a vision that grew to become known as House Against Hunger. Since 1987, when that first house was completed, other such projects have sprouted in Mennonite communities throughout the United States.

Leo Martin had his hands in the housing program with MCC. He began by approaching the relief organization with ideas about how to involve its constituency in hands-on fund raising projects. They liked Leo's ideas and offered him an assignment as Director of Resource Development.

"I traveled in Africa, India, and Bangladesh for a month as part of my orientation," Leo says. "My exposure to the needs in those countries helped me plan ways to involve Mennonites [MCC's constituency] in relief efforts."

Among Leo's ideas were the seeds for House Against Hunger. Leo heard about the house in Goshen and thought there was potential in his community to build such a house.

Leo made contacts among business people and builders near his home in Hagerstown, Maryland. Many showed interest, but were hesitant about whether such a large-scale project was feasible. Leo's goal was to build a house of donated materials with volunteer labor, so that most or all of the purchase price could be given to MCC hunger relief programs.

He found a kindred spirit in Mahlon Diller, a contractor in Shippensburg, Pennsylvania. Mahlon had a similar desire to use his building skills to benefit a cause he believed in. He agreed to oversee the building of a house and located a reasonably priced building lot.

Leo returned to earlier business contacts, and received $15,000 in donated materials. Customarily, two-fifths of a building's costs are for labor, which represented $40,000 in the cost of this proposed house. Mahlon and Leo lined up volunteer workers and hoped to net at least a $40,000 contribution from the sale of the house.

On the day of ground-breaking in early December, 35 volunteers arrived. In barn-raising fashion, the house was framed and under roof in two days.

The people who came to build the house were from a radius of 40 miles. They represented five different groups of Mennonites and 10 different churches. Someone observed that all the workers might not have felt comfortable worshiping together because of the diversity among them, but constructing the house was a way to build communication bridges between those different Mennonite and Brethren in Christ members.

A sign in the yard told passers-by that the proceeds from the house would be given to MCC for relief work in Bangladesh. As news traveled through the community, the coordinators received more donations of time and money.

"People like the hands-on nature of House Against Hunger," says Leo. "The houses provide a tangible way for people to use their abilities to benefit people all over the world."

Early one morning Leo called a retired farmer to see whether he wanted to join a carload of workers going to the building site. The man wasn't feeling well and decided not to go that day. The rest proceeded to Shippensburg and began their work. Several hours later the man arrived, saying that he started thinking about the hunger and poverty in the world and decided he didn't feel so bad in light of that.

Leo's goal was to have the house complete by April, five

months after it was begun, so it could be sold by the time of the Pennsylvania MCC Relief Sale. The house still needed some finishing touches, but the contract for sale was made prior to the Relief Sale, with all real estate services donated by a Brethren in Christ man. The house was sold for $105,000, clearing $86,000, rather than the projected $40,000, for MCC.

As a way of inviting other communities to participate in similar projects, Leo compiled a slide presentation which included current world hunger needs and pictures of the Shippensburg House Against Hunger.

"By showing the faces of people, giving names and telling stories, people feel more directly linked to the need at hand." He made presentations to Mennonite communities in Kansas, Pennsylvania, California, and Oregon. Each group responded with eagerness, but also reservation. The thought of building an entire house was overwhelming. But the success of the house in Indiana and the one in Shippensburg gave the needed incentive, and eventually houses sprung up in each of these areas.

When Leo first visited Kansas, the Mennonites he met were very committed to building a house for MCC. However, the state was in economic trouble that year with wheat and oil prices at record lows. When the economy improved a year later, plans began and a house was built.

A group in State Line, Pennsylvania, gathered enough people and supplies to frame and roof a house in one day. Leo brought video footage of that project to a meeting in Lancaster, Pennsylvania, where he hoped to generate interest for building a house. Twenty people came for his presentation. Enthusiasm ran high, and the group decided to build three houses rather than one.

The three houses went up—in Gap, Ephrata, and Elizabethtown—each under separate leadership. The Gap house included a work team of Mennonites and Amish, and was the first project where women were involved.

Recently, over 400 people volunteered to build a second house in Kansas. The house-building was a focal point in the community and became the "potbelly stove" of yesteryear when people gathered in the local hardware store to discuss the progress of the house.

"At numerous sites fathers came with their sons," says Leo. "In some cases the sons were quite young, but were eager to help and learn. Young contractors, who couldn't afford to donate materials, were glad to offer several days of volunteer help.

"A youth group near Chambersburg, Pennsylvania, held a fund-raiser supper to buy kitchen cabinets. Many people donated much more than the meal was worth and the youth raised $1,400.

"At one site a neighbor watched the frame of the house go up and asked why so many people were working on one house. When he heard the story, he was so impressed he asked if he could help. He sawed lumber all day."

Each year House Against Hunger raises between $500,000-$700,000 for hunger relief aid. The project unites young and old, men and women, Mennonites, Brethren in Christ, and Amish to build quality homes. Volunteers construct the frames, shingle the roofs, install windows, complete wiring and plumbing, drywall the rooms, paint woodwork, stain cabinetry, and supply meals. Twenty-four houses are complete and more are under construction. MCC uses the funds for programs in the United States and abroad for agricultural development, emergency food aid, and development of hunger relief programs.

My father started as a minister in a little urban church in Reading, Pennsylvania, in the fifties. In that era, neighborhood children were invited to attend Sunday school at the church, but few of their parents attended.

When my father first met Willie Mae Thomas she was a teenager with one child who came to church. She eventually had four children who all came to Sunday school. Her children really enjoyed coming to the church and to my parents' house, and Willie Mae wondered why.

One Sunday night she came to a foot-washing service at the church. She did not participate that evening, but closely observed. She was moved to tears by the words that were exchanged and the humble act of people washing each other's feet. My father explained the meaning behind footwashing, and she continued to ask questions.

After that she called my parents to ask more specific questions about our beliefs. She gradually came into the church and became a woman of faith. She was a Sunday school teacher for me and my brothers and sisters, and we all learned to know her as Sister Willie Mae. Willie Mae is now in her seventies and still attends the church and continues to minister to my siblings and me through letters.

Before Willie Mae began attending the church, her children were being cared for by my parents through the church programs and frequent visits in our home. She, in turn, became a pastor to their children. It was a flip-flop of caring. My parents could not have known when they met this woman that she would give so much to their children at some later time.

Aldine Musser
Bridgewater Corners, Vermont

Long Nights
of Mercy

*Joy has been asleep for only an hour when she is awakened by
the muffled sounds of her children, Nathaniel and Maria, crying.
Her weary body tells her to stay in bed, but she can picture them
scratching and bleeding, and so she climbs the stairs to give them
comfort. She sits on the bed beside Nathaniel, and he clings to
her for a moment. Maria comes to join them. The cream Joy
spreads on her son's arms, legs, and feet offers a small amount of
relief, and his sobbing subsides. Maria lays her head on her
mother's lap, and now Joy rubs Maria's dry and cracking skin
with the lotion. She prays while rubbing the small feet, legs, and
back, an unspoken transmittal of love through this gesture in
these late night hours. She has mercy for her children and wants
them to know they do not suffer alone. She cloaks them in the
love of God, even though she sometimes wonders how God can
allow them to lie awake at night in such pain.*

Joy and Elwood Yoder's children suffer from acute eczema, a
hereditary, but noncontagious skin disorder. Nathaniel never
had velvety soft skin like most newborns. He first showed signs
of skin irritation when he was six months old. Maria's symptoms
didn't appear until she was two and a half years old. The eczema
has fluctuated in severity, at times covering their bodies with
sore dry scabs that crack and bleed.

For the Yoders, eczema has provided an unusual window
through which to watch their children. They are constantly
aware of the physical pain Nathaniel and Maria suffer, and of
the emotional scars that might result. Joy and Elwood have
embodied the love of God for their children by staying beside
them when the hurting seems too much to bear. At the same
time, three different Mennonite communities have been a

God-like presence for all of them. When it seems they are standing in a permanent shadow, the gestures of family members and church friends personify God's love and involvement in their lives.

Nathaniel's eczema first appeared during a transition time for Joy and Elwood. They were about to move from Lancaster to Greencastle, Pennsylvania, where they would be closer to Joy's family and Elwood could explore his goal of enrolling in seminary.

Their years in Lancaster had been good ones. They were part of a local congregation, East Chestnut Street Mennonite Church, and both taught at Lancaster Mennonite High School. Friends from church became a surrogate family in the absence of relatives, and the Yoders intentionally lived beside friends in city row houses. In Greencastle, Joy's family members became their support network as they first began to realize Nathaniel's condition.

At first Nathaniel's sudden rash appeared to be an allergic reaction to dairy products. When it persisted, the Yoders sought medical help to relieve Nathaniel of his constant discomfort. Their doctor diagnosed the problem as eczema. The only known healer of the condition was time. No medication had been developed to control or eliminate the symptoms. Other children had outgrown eczema, and perhaps Nathaniel would, too.

The responsibility placed on Joy and Elwood was dizzying. Red, cracking sores covered Nathaniel's entire body—face, torso, arms, and legs. He found temporary relief by scratching, which, in turn, contributed to further irritation and bleeding. His suffering was especially apparent at night when he lay in bed sobbing and scratching at already open wounds.

The people of Joy's home church, Marion Mennonite, showed their concern through encouragement and prayer. In addition, they received regular letters and phone calls from Lancaster. These kind words lifted their morale. The knowledge that people upheld them in prayer helped Joy through the days that followed sleepless nights.

Each night a vigil began. Nights were long and taxing, especially for Joy who would get little sleep and go through the following day in a daze. Peers and intimate friends from Lancaster seemed to understand the weight of the constant night schedule. Regularly, people offered to keep Nathaniel overnight to give Joy and Elwood a break from the nightly routine. But they felt a responsibility to be the constant care-givers at night for their child. They knew it might be traumatic for Nathaniel to have many different people coming to comfort him in the night.

It was in December of Nathaniel's first year, that, for no apparent reason, he broke out head to toe in horrible red scabs and open sores. Word spread through the Greencastle and Lancaster communities, and Joy and Elwood knew people were praying for them. One Sunday a church member who worked in a local hospital suggested they take Nathaniel to Johns Hopkins University Hospital in Baltimore. The hospital had a teaching program for medical students. Because of the educational nature of the program, the expense was low, and the family was able to afford several trips for Nathaniel to be tested and photographed.

Joy and Elwood met regularly with a small group of families from the Marion Mennonite Church. Each member was a link of support when medical reports were discouraging or the night routine was especially draining.

When Nathaniel's condition persisted, the church deacon anointed him. Members of the church expressed their concern and helped as they could. However, few tangible things could be done.

Few Sundays went by when the pastor didn't mention Nathaniel in prayer. But Joy and Elwood couldn't help but ask, where is God in all of this? Certainly God was present in the love shown through these people. But the God they prayed to seemed to have turned his back.

When their eighth wedding anniversary approached, Elwood and Joy felt too exhausted to celebrate. Then mail arrived from a couple in Lancaster. Included with a letter of the latest news were details explaining that Joy and Elwood were to stay in a hotel on their anniversary. All accommodations were paid, and their friends would take care of Nathaniel.

The next summer the Yoders moved to Harrisonburg, Virginia, where Elwood enrolled at Eastern Mennonite Seminary and served as an intern pastor in the small country congregation of Cross Roads.

The nights continued to be very difficult, especially for Joy. Virginia's climate was humid and hot, and sweat was an additional irritant to Nathaniel's fragile skin. Although the family and friendship networks which they had established in Lancaster and Greencastle were painfully absent, neither Joy nor Elwood felt they had the energy to invest in new relationships. Once again, they had to explain that Nathaniel's skin rash was not contagious. But the members of the Cross Roads Church were receptive and accepting. Joining another small group of families helped Joy with the transition into a new community while Elwood adjusted to school life.

Joy wanted a second child. She wanted Nathaniel to have a companion, and maybe a second child would help her cope with some of the hardships of Nathaniel's eczema. But the question in the forefronts of their minds was what would be the chance that a second child would also have eczema? A nutritionist told them that the odds were slim.

Maria was born. She appeared to be a healthy baby with no immediate signs of skin disorder. Cross Roads women made a baby quilt and held a baby shower. A friend from Lancaster came to spend a week with Joy and help with the baby. Her car was a portable baby shower, overflowing with food and gifts from members of East Chestnut Street Mennonite. The generosity that continued to flow from a congregation they had not been part of for several years was overwhelming.

The year after they moved to Virginia, Nathaniel was unexpectedly hospitalized to have his tonsils removed. Elwood was in his second year of seminary, and their income was low. They only had major medical health insurance with a deductible that was several thousand dollars higher than the bill. Within a short time the seminary and Cross Roads Church worked together to pay three-fourths of the bill in conjunction with Mennonite Mutual Aid, the church's insurance company. Even Nathaniel, who was only three years old, observed the love coming from the people of Cross Roads. One Sunday as they approached the church building he exclaimed, "This is neat! We're going to church and all of our friends are inside."

In spite of the odds, Maria, too, began to show symptoms of eczema as a toddler. Her case was not as extreme as Nathaniel's, but additional demands were placed on Joy. Elwood tried to relieve Joy, but he had to store up energy for his studies and part-time work. When one child cried, the other often awakened. Joy could not allow herself to shut out their cries. Instead she would lie in bed picturing them itching and bleeding. Eventually she would roll out of bed to soothe them.

When Elwood completed his seminary studies, his pastoral work at Cross Roads ended. They transferred their membership to Zion Mennonite, where there was a greater number of families with children and more established programs. Again, they were invited to participate in a small group.

During a small group gathering on a hot summer night, Joy and Elwood mentioned that the heat was particularly hard on their children's skin condition. Afterward, a member of their small group asked several Sunday School classes to take part in an offering to help them purchase an air conditioner. The two classes raised more than $500. The air conditioner made a significant difference in the children's sleeping habits, and provided an extra boost for their weary parents.

But the caring did not stop with that. The church invited Joy and Elwood to share their story so the congregation could understand the implications of eczema within their family life. Speaking to the congregation has been both difficult and cathartic. Difficult for Joy, particularly. She says it would be easier for her to come to church, smile, and say everything is fine. Even when it isn't. Cathartic, for both, in the processing and sharing of pain with others. The people at Zion have freed them to be frank and open about their anger, pain, and disappointments, as well as acknowledging the stress this has added to their marriage. Others, too, have shared their own painful or difficult experiences, which has helped the Yoders feel less isolated in their situation.

In all the pain, Joy has focused her concern on Nathaniel's

and Maria's welfare. She has felt personal pressure and stress, but observing her children being mistreated by others is especially difficult. She knows she cannot protect them from harsh comments and questions. Yet, while it is one thing to struggle herself, it is quite another to see her children suffer day in and day out. How does Nathaniel feel when another child won't hold his hand? What can she say to Maria when she asks why God made her this way?

But Joy and Elwood are encouraged by offhand comments their children make in reference to God, friends, and themselves. Nathaniel grows weary of explaining what he "has" when children ask if it is chicken pox. But as his kindergarten year progresses, his teacher tells Joy that she forgets Nathaniel has eczema.

Close to Christmas, Nathaniel observed a painted Santa Claus on a restaurant window. "There's God!" he exclaimed. He pictured God as a jolly Santa that gives gifts. Joy's own picture of God has been altered with time. She tries to focus on God as unconditionally loving, but admits that she sometimes feels God has deliberately chosen not to answer her prayers. She is regularly reminded that people are praying for her, which is a reassurance of God's intentions not to abandon her or her children.

Elwood's perception of God has also changed. He still experiences God as loving, but has changed his understanding of what answer to prayer means. At any given time he knows that people from three different communities, Lancaster, Greencastle, and Harrisonburg are praying for their family. Yet, he experiences a darkness in his soul when he feels that God is moving too slowly or healing Nathaniel in a different way. Perhaps God has chosen healing as a process, not as an instantaneous happening. Over the five years Nathaniel has had eczema, he has experienced slow and gradual improvement.

A variety of emotions surface as the family looks forward to the arrival of a third child. Their anticipation of new life is tinged with some anxiety. It is feasible that this child may also carry the hereditary eczema that has caused so much suffering for Nathaniel and Maria. Joy knows she will love this child, regardless of its condition, but still she prays that it will be healthy. In contrast, Elwood anticipates the birth of the third child from a different perspective: as a profound statement of hope.

Despite the physical pain Nathaniel and Maria experience, they are still children with pervasive excitement and curiosity. Nathaniel wears a long sleeved winter shirt, so that the only sign of his ailment is the raw dry skin on his hands. His face is clear of eczema now, and the only markings are cavernous dimples that appear when he breaks through his shyness to smile. Maria's eczema is confined mainly to her legs and feet. Even in winter she dislikes wearing socks, which irritate and grab at the dry skin. She, too, appears shy, but exhibits equally delightful dimples when she returns a smile. They behave like children who are deeply loved—full of creativity, laughter, and joy.

A JOURNEY

Carl Keener was on of two children of Amos and Dorothy Keener. Carl was born in 1931. When he was only four months old, the keeners took him as a foster child, and ten years later they adopted him. Carl says that, during al lhis life, he experienced a deep acceptance, as though he were Amos and Dorothy's own biological child.

He felt this same acceptance at the Lititz Mennonite Church where his family attended. He experienced simple gestures that became powerful symbols of belonging. One of the most vivid of these was when he at with his Grandfather Hershey in church. "At some point in the served," Carl recalls, "Grandfather would invariable take my hand, give it a squeeze, leaving a piece of candy. I don't know if he ever ate candy, but that act sums up in a powerful way my early feelings of acceptance."

Later in Carl's childhood, his family moved and began attending the Hammer Creek Mennontie Church. The people were marked outwardly by plain clothing and a simple lifestyle, appearing rather rigid and stern. But for carl, these people proved to be inwardly remarkable. He experienced Hammer Creek as a warm congregation, exuding the very spirit of Christ.

Carl remembers that the congregation gave each individual space to grow and to become a useful person in the church and in the community. "For me," Carl says, "this meant the capacity and freedom to explore ideas without feeling condemned."

Carl liked books and studies more than farm work. He recalls that on one occasion he asked a visiting minister for his opinion of college. Although the minister felt there were inherent dangers in higher education, he said to Carl, "Get what you need." In those days, only a handful of young people from Hammer Creek went to college. "But," Carl says, "to the credit of our families and Hammer Creek, all of us stayed within the Mennonite Church."

Carl pursued higher education and eventually earned a Ph.D. He has been a professor of biology at the

Pennsylvania State University for 28 years and is an active member of the University Mennonite Church.

Two Roads
to College

Paul Schrock, 1950

Ryegrass harvesting had just begun in western Oregon, and Paul Schrock headed for the field on the tractor, pulling the combine in his wake. Windrows of ryegrass stalks formed golden stripes parallel to the horizon, their heads heavy with seeds. He was more intrigued by the book in his back pocket than the day's 12 hours of work, and he secretly wished that the machinery would break down. At least then he might have time to read a chapter of his book in the shade of the combine while Father fixed the equipment. The Schrock family was part of a small Mennonite community in the Willamette Valley of western Oregon. Two mountain ranges, the jagged and often snow-capped Cascades to the east, and the rolling green Coastal Range to the west, acted as literal and symbolic shields against the outside world. Life in the Valley was sustained by the fertile land and the meandering Willamette River, a tributary to the Columbia River that lay north. Life here could easily go on untouched by the outside world. Although there was limited personal contact with other Mennonites, a significant and regular contact crossed the mountains—the pages of church publications from Scottdale, Pennsylvania.

A children's periodical called *Words of Cheer* helped Paul feel connected to East Coast Mennonites, despite the geographic gap between them. When *Words of Cheer* published a letter he had written, Paul found another link in the form of a pen pal from Lancaster, Pennsylvania.

Oliver Zehr, 1932

Oliver Zehr's car wouldn't start. Short of walking or riding a horse, it was his only way to go to school, and on a cold morning like this neither of the other options was too enticing. Few of his friends were attending school anymore; most had joined their fathers on the farms that filled the Valley. So why not quit school now? There would always be time to finish later.

Paul, 1954

Paul's fascination with reading posed a bit of a problem with his parents. They wondered when he would get serious about farming and learn to make a living. But Paul had little interest in farming. His mind was on college. He had just graduated from Western Mennonite School and hoped to go to Eastern Mennonite College (EMC) in Harrisonburg, Virginia, in the fall. Paul's father, Melvin, recognized a glimmer of his younger self in his son. Melvin's generation had wanted to attend high school, and Melvin and his father had butted heads on that issue. Melvin's father had won their dispute. He did not begin high school until he was "of age."

Over the span of one generation the issue between father and eldest son progressed from high school to college. The value of education was not a debate confined to the Schrock family. Throughout Mennonite communities across the country, parents and children struggled over the benefits and dangers of higher education. When the time came, Melvin realized that he could not, in good conscience, forbid Paul to go to college.

On August 3, the day before Paul's nineteenth birthday, Melvin tried one last measure to keep him on the farm.

"Son, if you decide to stay and help out around here, I'll buy you a car."

A car to any 19-year-old is a powerful enticement. Paul couldn't help but consider the offer.

"But, if you decide to go to college," Melvin added, "I will begin to pay you wages. You can work as long as you like and take what you earn."

Oliver, 1943

Oliver had always hungered to see the world. Ten cycles of the farm year had passed since he left school, and he was ready for a change. Later, he couldn't pinpoint what provoked him to join the Navy, other than his profound desire to travel. The energy and vitality of youth is not always subject to reason.

The Construction Battalion of the Navy only took him as far as Camp Perry, Virginia, and he terminated after a year. On the way back to Oregon he stopped to work in a rural Mennonite community in Stark County, Ohio. As he traveled by bus to and from work, he recognized a fellow passenger whom he had seen in church on Sunday. Mary Helmuth was a graduate of Eastern Mennonite College and had recently moved to Ohio with her family.

World War II was coming to a close when Mary and Oliver were married and moved to Oregon.

Paul, 1954

By the end of August, Paul Schrock found himself with $48 in his pocket, riding east with five other people across the Cascade Mountains. He had made no admissions or financial arrangements with Eastern Mennonite College. Three days later he arrived in Virginia's Shenandoah Valley, woozy and half sick after driving, day and night, through a heat wave of over 100 degrees each day, without air conditioning.

Paul took freshmen tests, chose courses, set up finances, and moved into the dormitory. The College helped him secure a bank loan, and he earned $1 an hour in a tire shop close to the school.

But as the first semester progressed he began to have doubts about his decision to go to college. Things weren't as romantic and adventurous as he had imagined them to be. The uncertainty of finances added to his concerns. Paul became painfully aware that a debt was accumulating, and he still hadn't found a direction in his studies.

Oliver, 1955

Oliver had joined the railroad, making repairs. He felt fortunate to have regular work and shared his money on occasions when he became aware of a need.

Melvin Schrock had spoken with him during the summer, asking for financial help with his son Paul's college education. The timing hadn't been right then, but now the second semester was starting, and Oliver figured a college freshman would be needing money. He scrawled out a check and dashed off a quick letter. He had always wanted to go to college, so why shouldn't he help someone else who had the opportunity? The words of Jesus came to mind, "As much as you have done for the least of these, you have done it unto me." This was how he preferred to help someone, person-to-person.

Paul, 1955

It was a discouraging week. Paul sat at his desk with a pencil between his teeth, staring at the words he had just written. He wondered what his parents would think when they got this letter. He continued to write, telling them about his debts and his feeling of not understanding why he was here or what to study. He had determined that college was not for Paul Schrock. If they would just send him some money, he would buy a bus ticket and return to the farm.

But the prospect of returning to Oregon wasn't satisfying either. Being a farmer had no more appeal now than it had before. The letter lay on the corner of his desk. He had no money, not even three cents for the stamp. Several days later, the letter still on the desk, Paul found an envelope in his student mailbox. The name "Oliver Zehr" was penciled in an almost illegible scrawl above an Oregon return address.

Paul remembered Oliver as a distant relative and friend of the family. He was a man who did some farming, but also worked on repairing the railroad. Oliver Zehr was not a leader in the church and, in some ways, existed on the fringes of church life. Why would he be writing to him? Paul couldn't guess. But to his amazement, a $300 check was enclosed with a short letter. The writing was the unpolished script of a man who had not been able to finish school.

Dear Paul,

I want you to know that I believe in you and I believe in Christian education. I am enclosing a check to help with your school expenses. You don't have to pay it back to me. If you ever are able to pay it back, pass it on to somebody else who needs help in their education.

> *Yours,*
> *Oliver Zehr*

This was such an unexpected and dramatic development that Paul reassessed his situation. If God had inspired Oliver to send the money, Paul figured he should continue to pursue a degree. Oliver's gesture bridged a gap Paul couldn't cross on his own. It was the catalyst that allowed Paul to continue at EMC and to begin to shape his future.

Oliver, 1975

Oliver would turn 60 next week. He had found it difficult to continue working since his hip replacement surgery, and the railroad finally recommended that he retire. After 30 years, he was free to do something different. His truck guided him down the familiar roads home—he could almost drive this route with his eyes closed. For some reason, the high school building stood out that day, catching his thoughts off-guard. He pulled into the parking lot without hesitation and within moments was addressing the principal, requesting admittance to the high school.

The principal was taken aback. This had never happened before. What made this 60-year-old man think he could just pick up where he left off in 1934, and how would teenagers respond to him?

This was not the only change Oliver was contemplating. Lately the rules of his home church felt claustrophobic. With each step he took, he felt watched and criticized. On Sunday someone had remarked that the belt he wore was not as suitable as suspenders. Another point of contention revolved around the retirement pension Oliver would receive after working for 30 years on the railroad. The church felt he should refuse the pension and allow them to support him. The church leaders were suspicious of further education and responded negatively to Oliver's desires to finish school.

Today he stood in the office of the local high school, ready to cut new paths. The education details were attended to, and Oliver joined the Central Linn High School junior class.

The principal's worries proved to be unfounded. Oliver consistently made the honor roll and was elected vice president of the student body. He graduated in the spring of 1977.

Oliver's goal to see the world stayed with him. That summer he and Mary took a trip to Europe, celebrating his high school graduation. And the Zehrs moved their membership to another local Mennonite church.

Paul, 1960

Paul returned to the EMC campus as a representative of the Mennonite Publishing House in Scottdale, Pennsylvania. His years as the college newspaper editor had led him into his editing job, and he enjoyed returning to EMC to recruit students for summer internships and postgraduate jobs in publishing.

The College asked him to address the student body in their morning chapel gathering. He looked out to the sleepy faces and then over to the college president, John R. Mumaw, who was seated next to him on the platform. Amazement passed over their faces, while each recalled how strained their relationship had sometimes been during Paul's enrollment at EMC.

Paul flashed back to an evening in the dormitories on the west side of the administration building when he threw a pair of tennis shoes out a third floor window. He intended to scare somebody below, but one of the shoes bounced off a window ledge into the open window of the president's office. Somehow Paul was identified as the culprit and soon found himself standing in front of John R. Mumaw. Paul had been there before after several other scrapes with the rules.

In an administrative manner Mumaw said, "Paul, I'm sorry that in years to come, I'll need to remember this situation." Impertinently, Paul replied, "J.R., I'm sorry that in years to come I will have to remember this about the College."

Both men chuckled inwardly at the memory, as Paul stepped to the podium.

Oliver, 1965

The letter that arrived from Paul Schrock took Oliver as much by surprise as his check had previously startled Paul. This time Paul had enclosed a check and suggested the name of a student who needed funds. Paul related that he now was working at the Mennonite Publishing House in Scottdale, Pennsylvania, and was married to June Bontrager of Alden, New York. Had it not been for Oliver's check, he would likely be working on the family farm. He thanked Oliver again for giving him a second chance to stay in college.

Oliver passed the money along to the student Paul suggested.

Oliver, 1982

With a high school diploma under his belt (not suspenders!), Oliver took steps to attend college, a goal that had earlier seemed unattainable. His application to a local community college was accepted.

He was delighted to open the volumes that filled the college library and fill his own head with the history of medieval Europe. He earned an Associate of Arts Degree in Humanities in the spring of 1982. He and Mary celebrated this achievement with a trip to Alaska.

The two-year program only whetted Oliver's appetite for still more education, so he continued his studies in history at Oregon State University. During his enrollment he participated in a three-week exchange program to Ecuador, in another effort to expand his cultural awareness. Health problems and several surgeries delayed his graduation until 1989, when he turned 74 years old.

Paul, 1993

During Paul's more than 30 years at Mennonite Publishing House, he has worked in many editorial and administrative positions, starting as assistant editor of *Gospel Herald,* the weekly magazine of the denomination. Within two years he began a nine-year stint as editor of the children's paper, *Words of Cheer,* the same paper he read as a child in Oregon. He founded the magazine, *Purpose,* and developed Christian education materials. Presently he is responsible for both the Herald Press book publishing program and the congregational literature division of Mennonite Publishing House.

Paul recalls that a second check arrived, and perhaps a third, during his college years, so that the total amount Oliver shared with him was substantial. He remains grateful to Oliver for the financial help that enabled him to graduate from college and pursue a writing and editing career.

Oliver, 1993

Life in the Willamette Valley is less isolated now than it once was. Oliver and Mary Zehr still live among the ryegrass fields that lie on each side of the river in the thriving Willamette Valley. The Valley air is pure; the cold river water, clean.

The mountain ranges remain a physical barrier to the happenings beyond them, but modern media penetrates them more easily now. Though Paul M. Schrock now resides on the East Coast, his words are circulated among his home community on the pages of Mennonite Publishing House materials that still cross the Cascade Mountains. Among his readers is Oliver Zehr.

Anne McElfresh was director of social services at the Jackson County Welfare Department in Jackson, Ohio. Her father left her a small fortune in stock and she owned a nice home on the best street in town.

She cared deeply for all the poor people who came to her with their needs. Often welfare benefits were exhausted but Anne never turned anyone away. Many times folks took advantage of her generosity, but Anne always helped, fearing she might turn someone away who was genuinely in need. Eventually, she gave away her entire inheritance.

One day soon after I became pastor at Hillside Mennonite Chapel, my wife, Isabel, and I went to Anne's office. We were seeking assistance for a family we were helping. We explained that I had gone to the family's home with some groceries, only to discover the woman had nothing to cook with. I returned home to raid our kitchen for pots and pans and a skillet. Isabel also told her about the twin babies we were caring for until their mother could get on her feet.

Anne talked about how her own church was spending a large sum of money for stained glass windows, of which she disapproved. She began attending Hillside Chapel and soon made the decision to move her membership. She became a champion of human rights and peace, writing multitudes of letters to the local paper, representatives, and senators. She was the conscience of our church. In addition, she taught a Sunday school class of children. When we remodeled the church basement she and her students requested their room be left as it was. They did not wish to have new carpets while some children did not have enough to eat.

Anne was a faithful and active member for 20 years until she died. Before her death she expressed concern to me about the $1,000 she had in the bank to cover final expenses. She knew there were hungry children who needed it. The editor of the local paper remembered her in his comments:

On Saturday afternoon a quiet and very nice memorial service was held at the Hillside Chapel for the late Anne McElfresh. Anne's four children and family were joined by many friends for some singing, scripture reading and many of those present told of the influence Anne had on their lives. It was a gentle, low-key heartwarming devotional time, mirroring the life of this fine lady.

Jim and Isabel Mullet
Jackson, Ohio

They Asked
Me Three Times

Marianne Mellinger today co-pastors a Mennonite church in the Germantown section of Philadelphia.

I began my journey into ministry while serving with the Mennonite Board of Missions in London, England, between 1977 and 1981. It was there that I wrote and delivered my first sermon, led worship, and did some teaching in our small Mennonite fellowship. My years in London were the beginning, but in retrospect I can name several experiences from my childhood in the late fifties and early sixties that also contributed to that journey.

For a young girl to feel a call to ministry in my childhood congregation was like being called to walk on the moon. I never considered it a possibility. However, I felt affirmation from my parents to pursue whatever vocation I chose. It was important to them that their daughters, as well as their son, be educated. While my parents were strong, faithful Christians, I experienced my family as being more on the fringe than in the center of the church. During mealtime we often discussed church life and the Sunday morning sermon. And I learned to appreciate a variety of viewpoints. My parents were also active in public school and community organizations. They especially loved music, and all five of us children played piano and a musical instrument. We attended concerts, and on occasion took in an opera in Philadelphia. Because my mother's extended family was mostly non-Mennonite, family gatherings included aunts, uncles, and cousins from several different denominations.

In 1966 I began my first year at Goshen College where several relatives taught and my other siblings had attended. My experience in college was an important growing period in my life.

My home community felt stifling, parochial, and static. Attending college in another area provided me with the distance I needed to broaden my views of the church and the world. I came to terms with who I was as an individual and developed a new image of God as a God of justice, which tied in with the Civil Rights Movement and the Vietnam War.

I graduated from Goshen College in 1970 with a degree in History Education and was married shortly afterward. My husband, Bob, and I lived in an intentional community with several other couples, and we soon started our family. Between our first two children I attended classes at Associated Mennonite Biblical Seminaries with no clear career goal in mind. I found the classes stimulating, but my after-class energies went into life within our community household. The community was a lively environment where all of us worked as a network to meet each other's needs. By 1974 our community began a small congregation, called Assembly, on the campus of Goshen College. My relationships in the community, involvement in the fledgling congregation, and my seminary learnings stretched me spiritually.

Three years later Mennonite Board of Missions asked us to go to England to direct the London Mennonite Center. We went in August of 1977, shortly before our third child was born.

At the time the Mennonite Center was a student facility with a resource center and book department focusing on Anabaptist history and peace and justice concerns. Bob and I shared parenting responsibilities, and I worked at developing the resource center.

The Mennonite Fellowship we attended was small and everyone contributed. I was asked to give a sermon and enjoyed the preparation, research, and writing, but it didn't seem particularly significant at that time.

I was enriched by the worship diversity we were exposed to in England. Along with the Mennonite Fellowship meetings, we attended Anglican evensongs, Quaker meetings, and services in several other denominations. We participated in several weekend conferences with church leaders in different parts of England. One such weekend had particular impact on me. The conference was held at a community in Devon. Our children were six months, two and a half, and four at the time, and I was exhausted, rarely getting a full night of sleep. The community hosting the conference offered wonderful hospitality. They brought all of their guests tea in bed in the morning. It was one of the most wonderful gifts I have ever received and made me realize the importance of hospitality. Extending hospitality to someone is both a witness and an offering. That is how I experienced it in that English community.

The last year we were in London was a time of conflict in our Mennonite Fellowship. I found myself caught in the middle without the spiritual resources to mediate. I started to seek out reading materials in that area and began an internal journey which continued when I returned to the United States in 1981. We moved to the outskirts of Philadelphia; Bob enrolled in a Ph.D. program and I tried to get re-acclimated to North American culture. It was a hard year. I didn't want to be here, but I wasn't sure where I should be. I did a lot of reading, journal-writing, and reflecting on who I was. My relationship with God was not intimate. It wasn't that I didn't believe in God; I just didn't find God to be very important to me.

Several experiences stand out from that time. A friend in London gave me a copy of the T.S. Eliot play, *The Cocktail Party,* as a going-away gift. A cocktail party is perhaps the height of superficiality, but Eliot uses this setting to address spirituality and how people relate to one another. I thought about relationships that were born out of pain and brokenness rather than the superficiality of much that we call life.

About that time our church asked Bob and me to lead Advent worship. The invitation gave me an opportunity to express creatively in worship what I was experiencing spiritually.

Despite my uncertainties, I stayed close to the church. I started seminary again and was resource person in Christian education and worship for our local conference.

In a church history class I traced the movement of women in the church from the center of activity in the early church of the first century (New Testament and extra New Testament documents record that women preached and baptized and were in leadership roles) to the fifth century when they were involved primarily behind convent walls. I reflected on my own experience in the church, and I began to think about a relational theology where justice is central.

When I graduated from seminary, I still thought pastoral ministry was an impossible dream. Some of my professors encouraged me to switch denominations so I could pastor, but that didn't feel right to me.

It seemed more unlikely that I would ever be a pastor when Bob and I separated in 1988. One of the gifts the Germantown congregation, where we were members, offered me during that time was acceptance. I was always actively involved in worship leading and planning, and had given an occasional sermon, but throughout the separation and divorce I chose to be on the fringe. I wasn't ready to leave the Mennonite church, nor was I able, because of what I was going through, to be centrally involved. I am most grateful to the church for allowing me to remain peripheral then. I think it is critical that the Mennonite church acknowledge that there are times in people's lives when they need to move in or out of the church. I was blessed by being allowed to stay on the edge.

During the divorce, I realize that people wanted to be supportive but didn't know how. At the same time, I didn't know what to ask for. I wasn't afraid to ask; I just didn't know what I needed. I see now that what I needed was distance.

Our break-up threatened other married couples in the church. I'm sure some people thought, "If this can happen to them after 20 years, can it happen to me?" Others had looked to us as models for living and raising our children in the city. Well, that exploded. I couldn't blame them for feeling threatened. I would have felt the same way, too.

I resigned from my position in the local conference, not because I thought I would be fired, but because I assumed that some congregations would choose not to use my resources. I didn't have the energy to fight that battle. I wanted to do church work, but felt I should do so outside of the Mennonite church at that time. So I entered a chaplaincy program, a healthy transition for me. Chaplains, like pastors, are usually licensed by their denomination, and I was concerned about whether the Mennonite church would license me. The local conference had no chaplaincy license but agreed to develop one. In the process, they developed two separate licenses—one for chaplains and one for pastors.

I gradually began to move back into the activities of the church. And I received affirmation and encouragement from members of my congregation. As I became more involved, I had more energy to lead worship when I was asked. I thoroughly enjoyed preparing for and then leading worship.

After I had worked as a chaplain for a few years, I was approached several times by leaders of my congregation at Germantown to consider being a pastor there. Twice I said no because I knew it would be a major hassle for the conference to ordain a divorced person. Being a woman pastor was no longer the issue, because several other women had been ordained before that time. But neither was I sure that I wanted to make the shift from layperson to leader within my own congregation. Furthermore, I was thoroughly enjoying being a chaplain, and so many changes had already happened in my life—separation, divorce, job changes. I needed stability.

But when I was asked for the third time, I felt I needed to take the call seriously. For the first time, I was ready to be open to their call. It seemed like we as a congregation had gone through a sort of wilderness time, not knowing where we were going. We had grown too large for our meeting house and were renting space for our worship services. At the time I was asked to be a pastor, the church was deciding where to look for a permanent building and what sort of presence the congregation wanted to be in that community.

I still assumed there would be trouble with my credentialing at the conference level in relation to my marital status, but with the strong affirmation from the congregation, and the support of some conference leaders, I felt ready to take that step. Unfortunately, the issue became bigger than I had anticipated, culminating in a daylong delegate session. Because I was the candidate, it was hard for me to separate myself from the "issue," which others tried very hard to do. It was not an easy time, but eventually my licensing for pastoral ministry was approved.

The other co-pastor and I share preaching, and I am responsible for the worship committee and pastoral care. I work two-thirds time at the church and am a therapist one-half time at a local counseling agency.

Somewhat to my surprise, I thoroughly enjoy being a pastor. I love the diversity of things that I do. Writing a sermon requires discipline and hard work. I am being stretched as I plan, lead, and participate in worship. I also receive from the congregation. I'm not just giving, giving, giving.

When 20-year-old Rod found out that his friend Mike had cancer, he couldn't believe his ears. It was inconceivable to him that someone his age could die. He wanted to be with Mike, but didn't always know how or what to say as he searched for answers for both of them. This was new territory; neither had traveled this road before. Rod worked through his own feelings and questions while staying close to Mike. Rod's family supported him through his struggles and ministered to Mike and his family.

I am Rod's pastor, and he asked me to meet with Mike. I tried to help him sort through his questions about life and death. Eventually he came to a place of acceptance and peace. Throughout Mike's illness our church family prayed for Mike and for Rod. It was a two-year journey from the doctor's diagnosis until Mike died. I conducted his funeral, and others from our church provided music for the service and a meal afterwards. Mike's family expressed their gratefulness. It was truly a journey for all of us together.

Ray Landis
Edmonton, Alberta

UNHEARd Lullaby

Pam and Roger Rutt were overjoyed with the birth of their daughter, Katelyn. She was beautiful. One of the nurses said to Pam, "Do you know that the doctor gave Katelyn a perfect 10 on the test used for assessing the health of newborn babies? That is really rare."

"Stating it mildly," Pam says, "we were thrilled."

During the coming months, the Rutts thoroughly enjoyed Katelyn's growth and development. She received another excellent report at her 15-month check-up. Pam came home and thankfully wrote, "The doctor said, 'Very healthy baby,'" in Katelyn's baby book.

During the next several days, however, Pam had a growing uneasiness because Katelyn was not yet talking. She mentioned her concern to friends who assured her that in a few months she'd wish Katelyn didn't talk so much.

But the Rutts' worry continued. Finally, Pam called the doctor and expressed her anxiety. He asked that she bring Katelyn in for a hearing test. The doctor made a few sounds behind Katelyn's head, but she made no response. "This pushed my anxiety sky-high," Pam says, "but I was in denial. I wanted to believe the doctor when he said Katelyn might have an ear infection that could be cleared up with medication." However, he proposed that the Rutts take Katelyn to an ear, nose, and throat specialist for a second opinion. Pam made the appointment. "At this point," Pam reflects, "I was no longer in total denial. I knew something was wrong, but hoped it was nothing serious."

That evening Roger's parents came to visit, and Pam told them about Katelyn's visit to the doctor. Roger's father tried getting Katelyn's attention from different parts of the room, and Pam clearly remembers him saying, "I'm not convinced she can hear." Pam's defenses began to crack, and for the first time she began to ask, "Can it really be true that our baby is deaf?" The question weighed heavily upon her.

That weekend the Rutts met with their small support group from church. By then Pam and Roger knew that something was wrong and shared the news of the week with the group. Everyone was shocked. Everyone cried.

Pam remembers rocking Katelyn to sleep that night. "In my spirit, I knew something was wrong and that I had to bury my dreams of a healthy baby. I felt that the baby in my arms was a stranger, a baby I didn't know. My little girl was in perfect health. But this baby's health was far from perfect. I always sang to my baby, but this baby couldn't hear me sing. I cried and cried. This was the song the baby in my arms 'heard' that night as she fell asleep."

The next morning was Sunday and, as was their custom, the Rutts attended East Chestnut Street Mennonite Church. They still had no definite confirmation that Katelyn was deaf, but wanted to share their grief with the congregation. "We realized in a new way the value of a church family that cares deeply about one another's trials and burdens," Roger recalls. "We were struck by the fact that we are not simply a group of people who move casually in and out of each other's lives, but a community of faith with hearts of compassion. It was this realization that gave us the freedom to share. As we did, the congregation wept with us."

The following day the specialist confirmed that Katelyn had a profound hearing loss. Only with prolonged therapy could they ever expect her to speak and to develop what little hearing she had.

"I was very angry," Pam says. "Angry at myself that I didn't pick up the problem sooner, and angry at God for letting this happen to us. I was also angry at the specialist who wrote 'deafness' so matter-of-factly on Katelyn's records and offered no emotional support. And I was angry at the world—the people we passed on our way home from the doctor. How could they go on with their life when my whole world was crashing in?"

Even as Roger and Pam felt the heaviness of the long road ahead, a small ray of hope began to break. Some acquaintances had a hearing-impaired daughter, so Pam called the mother and they talked for over an hour. She was a helpful listener.

Later, Roger and Pam met with the family and received their first education in options for Katelyn. They helped guide the Rutts into auditory/verbal speech therapy. It was encouraging to see what the therapy had done for their daughter.

Another source of hope came through Nancy, a deaf seminary student who stayed with the Rutts for several months during her pastoral internship at the First Deaf Mennonite Church. Nancy functioned gracefully and easily, enabling them to imagine how Katelyn could develop.

After much prayer and counsel, the Rutts chose to have Katelyn learn to speak and listen with a hearing aid before learning sign language. They enrolled her in an auditory (hearing) speech therapy program at the Helen Beebe Clinic in Easton, Pennsylvania, one of the top auditory/verbal therapy centers in the country. The method of therapy would develop what residual hearing Katelyn had and discourage lip-reading. Katelyn would go there two times a week for an hour session, in addition to daily therapy at home.

Roger and Pam were one of the few couples in Lancaster County who chose auditory therapy for their deaf child. This decision caused some tension between them and the local Mennonite deaf community. Many deaf Mennonites were upset that they weren't teaching Katelyn to sign. "At first I was resistant to having her learn sign language," says Pam. "But now I want her to have it as a second language. It is part of the deaf culture and will make it easier for her to communicate with her deaf peers. We chose to have her learn to speak first because it is more difficult, and by starting young she will be able to do better. She can learn to sign later."

Katelyn began wearing hearing aids, and Roger and Pam could see her responding to sound. She loved therapy and eagerly anticipated each trip. For several months, people from East Chestnut Street took turns driving the two hours to therapy with Pam and Katelyn. A number of the members read a book on the therapy program and were able to understand how the Rutts were working with Katelyn's needs. Katelyn needed specific toys for therapy. They told the congregation what she needed, and people loaned them a wide variety of toys. Others gave a helping hand by baby-sitting older brother, Jason, on Katelyn's therapy days.

Eventually, Roger and Pam learned that Katelyn was no longer progressing in therapy. The staff at Beebe advised her parents to find a program that better fit Katie's needs. They wrestled over what to do. Leaving Lancaster would mean leaving behind family, lifelong friends, and a special church community. But, staying would deprive Katelyn of the oral education they desired for her.

In the late winter, Roger and Pam visited deaf schools in Missouri, California, Pittsburgh, and Philadelphia. They were impressed with a small Catholic school for the hearing impaired in Pittsburgh. The school taught lipreading, in addition to listening. It felt like the right place for Katie, and the Rutts returned home at peace about moving there.

Originally they planned to move that summer, but they began to wonder whether they should relocate immediately. A few days after their visits, they had invited their pastor and his wife, Mel and Marie Thomas, for dinner. "It was perfect timing," says Roger. "We were able to share our dilemma with them and they listened. Mel told us that he would be sorry to see us leave, but he thought we should go. That was helpful for us, because we knew our families would have a hard time encouraging us to leave. Shortly after that we told them of our plans to move."

"Another pull to Pittsburgh was that there was a Mennonite church there," says Pam. "I called the pastor at Pittsburgh Mennonite to tell him we were planning to come in March and didn't know anyone. We planned that the children and I would go for a three-month trial period, and, if all went well, we would move.

"The church very graciously and kindly helped us. Since the move was temporary, people loaned us furniture, kitchenware, and odds and ends. They also gave us food and brought us meals. I was pregnant during that time, and they were helpful in recommending doctors and a hospital. They plugged us into everything they did, and helped us feel at home. Our Catholic neighbors knew nothing of Mennonites and observed, 'You

Mennonites really take care of each other!' I think we knew that things would work out there, and those three months confirmed that."

Katelyn's school proved to offer the sort of instruction they wanted. At kindergarten age she was already learning to read, and, although she was language delayed, the world of books offered a new form of entertainment and learning. "At a parent-teacher conference we learned that Katelyn tested in the gifted range," says Pam. "She has a lot of potential and is one of the top students in her class."

At seven, Katelyn is bubbly and energetic like other children her age. She is just beginning to understand that her way of communication is different from other people, which reflects in her face when she tries to talk with someone and they don't understand.

Roger and Pam have learned the power of conversing with God through the community of faith. They continue to ask the church to join them in prayer, not for Katelyn's healing, but for wisdom in knowing how to draw out and cultivate the gifts that lie within her. At other times they wonder whether they are shortchanging Katelyn by not asking for her healing. Roger continues to struggle with how to pray for a situation like his daughter's. "It is still unresolved for me. We don't know what to ask for because we don't understand why a child is born deaf. No one knows how to pray.

"No congregation is a group of experts on caring and sharing. Each family situation is different, and when someone has a problem the congregation should not simply 'plug in' the same formula that worked with someone else. We all have burdens. It's simply a matter of acknowledging them and discerning how to help each other. It is difficult to maintain the momentum for such caring , but to do less is to cave in to self-help individualism rather than to joyfully accept the challenge of bearing one another's burdens."

"Through helping Katelyn to discover life, we have begun to rediscover life ourselves," Pam says. "We want this process to continue as we work together with the faith community to care sensitively for each other."

Although we had both been Christians for many years, during our first six years of marriage we didn't find a church where we felt we belonged. Barbara grew up in a Presbyterian congregation, and I, John, grew up in a family that didn't attend church at all.

For several years Barbara and I were involved in the charismatic movement. Later I served as an interim pastor for a Salvation Army congregation and directed a community center in a black neighborhood in Dayton, Ohio. Neither the Salvation Army or the charismatic movement offered us what we were looking for.

In December of 1980 I was transferred to Cincinnati. Thus began a miserable several weeks of looking for a new church. While Christmas shopping in a local shop, I noticed a plaque with a quote by Menno Simons. I had read about Anabaptists and suspected that the shop proprietor must be a Christian. The owner introduced himself as Ervin Stutzman, pastor of a Mennonite church near to where we lived.

We visited the Mennonite Christian Assembly (now called New Beginnings Mennonite Fellowship) and soon felt the warmth of these Mennonite Christians. Glen and Ellen Yoder and Ervin and Bonnie Stutzman, the pastoral couples, offered us acceptance and Christ-centered teaching. Another couple in the church nurtured and cared for our two young sons. What mattered to these people was our commitment to Jesus Christ; we weren't required to accept some denominational culture, Mennonite or otherwise. We were impressed with the balance between solid evangelical theology and a concern for low-income minority peoples. Furthermore, we saw an expression of Christianity modeled that did not throw out creativity and education. Perhaps what convinced us that we had found our niche in the Body of Christ was the evening we participated in a "Guess Who's Coming to Dinner?" meal. The hospitality and good Mennonite cooking of our hosts won our hearts and stomachs!

That was over 12 years ago. Now a third son, a nursing degree, and an ordination later, we find ourselves in the North Central Mennonite Conference in northwestern Minnesota, pastoring the Strawberry Lake Mennonite Church and ministering in the chaplaincy and hospice programs of a rural Catholic hospital. We belong to a warm and caring fellowship in which many other wandering Christians have found a home in the Mennonite corner of the Body of Christ.

John and Barbara Burroughs
Ogema, Minnesota

Shouts From God

Betsy Martin's life took a surprising turn one December night. This verse has sustained her—"Now we know that if the earthly tent we live in is destroyed, we have a building from God, an eternal house in heaven, not built by human hands."
—II Corinthians 5:1, NIV

On Saturday, December 9, my husband Ike and I left our home in Leola, Pennsylvania, in a used school bus en route to Miami, Florida. Our daughter Dolores and her husband had purchased the bus in July for the church he pastors in Costa Rica. The title transfer was completed after four months, so we decided to deliver the bus to Miami before the harsh winter weather began. From there the bus would be shipped to its final destination.

The sidewalks and roads were slick with ice and snow. As we climbed into the bus, Ike commented, "Isn't it interesting that so many people have said they will pray for us on this trip. Even the lady we bought the bus from said she would pray."

After two long days of travel we finally left the snow behind. When we arrived in Miami on Sunday night we were thankful for our safe journey, in spite of treacherous driving conditions.

Throughout our marriage, Ike and I have taken turns leading devotions every night. Even though it was my turn that night and Ike was exhausted, he read aloud from the Bible and led in prayer.

We needed to make an early start on Monday so we could finalize details for shipping the bus. We needed to make arrangements with the shipping company, acquire a bill of lading, set up inspections with the highway patrol, and reserve a rental car for ourselves after the bus was gone.

By five o'clock that evening we had not yet been cleared with customs, so we decided to find a motel and a place to eat. Immediately after checking into a Day's Inn near the freeway, we crossed the street to a Chinese restaurant. The strains of

"Joy to the World" filled the room as we gave our order. While we ate, Ike pointed out a young girl standing by the entrance and speculated about whether she might be there for security. Everyone else in the restaurant ate quietly without noticing or finding this unusual, so we quickly dismissed the thought.

The sun had gone down and the neighborhood looked deserted when we stepped outside at 6:30 p.m. To our surprise we found the iron gate to our motel locked, so we proceeded to the back of the motel where there was another gate. Just as we turned the corner, two young men stepped out and blocked our way, demanding my purse. The precious bus title and papers that had taken months to acquire had been in my purse all day. Not wanting to lose them, Ike protested, "No, don't take that." Before I could open my mouth to offer them my money, one of them put a small handgun to Ike's head and pulled the trigger.

Horrified, I watched Ike crumple to the pavement as the two men grabbed my purse and ran. I heard my own scream as though it had come from someone other than myself, and fell beside Ike to check for a heartbeat, though what I saw gave me little hope.

Within minutes a crowd emerged from what had appeared to be an empty neighborhood. Although I later learned that racial tension was acute in that area, a large African-American man came and put his arm around me, gently leading me away to shield me from the scene. There were swarms of police. One of them helped me into a police car and put his jacket around my shaking body as I slipped into shock.

An ambulance arrived and the crew members knelt over Ike, trying to save him. I prayed desperately that God would let him live. The squealing sirens of the ambulance that rushed Ike to the hospital faded away as the police car took me in another direction to the homicide office of the Miami Police Department. There I learned that we had unknowingly stumbled into a high crime and drug trafficking area of the city.

The police department was a blur of mug shots and questions. The detectives did everything they could for me and made all the necessary phone calls. An hour after I arrived, the hospital informed me that Ike was dead. By this time I was too numb to cry, and I sat stunned at the detective's desk while he tried to think of the right thing to say. He vented his frustration and anger that such a thing should happen to a man like my husband. Although I experienced extreme pain and confusion, I also felt a deep sense of God.

The detective asked me if I would live alone now. My natural response was that I had my faith in God, my family, and church to support me. As I spoke these words, I didn't realize how profoundly and incredibly true they were.

I have often felt frustrated with myself for finding it so difficult to witness in an effective way. But somehow that night it seemed natural to share my faith. The detective listened, although the words seemed foreign to him. His reaction to Ike's murder was that the men should be caught and given the death sentence. I, in turn, felt no hatred toward them. I wondered what kinds of homes they had come from and what forces had gripped their lives,causing them to kill somebody. In spite of my great loss, I knew I had so much more than they did.

Before I left the police station the detective drove to the Day's Inn to get my suitcases from the rental car. When he returned he held up an envelope and said, "Look what I found." It was the bus title and all the papers I had assumed were in my purse. They were on the back seat of the locked car. I don't know how they got there, but they were a sign to me that God was still in control.

Ike's sister, Mary Alice, arrived from Immokalee, Florida, about four hours after she was contacted. She had come with her pastor, his wife, and another friend. They had driven through the night to take me back to Immokalee.

There was little time the next day to grieve. So many things needed to be taken care of. I spent most of the day on the telephone making funeral plans, arranging the release of Ike's body from the hospital, and dealing with the still unshipped bus. In between calls, the phone rang with police and reporters. A Christian radio station in Miami was inundated with calls from listeners wanting to know what they could do to help. Later, I received $1,000 from their listening audience. Another caller said he wanted me to know that people and churches all over Miami were praying for our family. People from Immokalee also came to the house to offer their condolences and help.

At four o'clock in the afternoon on Tuesday, less than 24 hours after the shooting, I left for the airport with Mary Alice. Just as we were leaving her house, the detectives called to say that two different airlines had offered free flights to Lancaster for me and Ike's body.

Back in Pennsylvania, family members assured me that the Lancaster reporters handled the story with a great deal of compassion and sensitivity. Our children had given a tribute to their father on three television interviews. I couldn't bear to watch the news videotapes or read the newspaper articles until several weeks later.

All of our children were together except our daughter Dolores and her husband Martin, who would arrive from Costa Rica the next day. We hugged, talked, cried, and read the Bible together, visualizing Dad in heaven with God. That night we all spread out on the family room floor so we could be close together through the night. I hadn't slept since Sunday night and was able to fall into a deep sleep. Although I awoke early in the morning (and did so for many mornings afterward), I was always able to fall asleep quickly. Friends told me later that they lay awake those nights, praying that I could sleep. God answered their prayers, and I was able to get the rest I needed to take me through those exhausting, difficult days.

My first days at home were packed with activity. The first morning, Lancaster City police came to the house to draw a composite of the men who had killed Ike. By 9 a.m. reporters were calling to request interviews. Dolores and her family arrived, in the swell of flowers, food, and friends that also came through the door of our home. Also, that day an African-American minister from Miami called to say how badly the black Christian community felt that black men were responsible for Ike's death. He said that the ministers were banding together to pray for us. The County Commissioner offered his condolences and prayers, as well as those of his Christian friend, the Dade County Commissioner in Miami. Lastly, a call came from the manager of the Day's Inn who repeated over and over how sorry he was.

The Miami Police Department detective had never seen a homicide case like this one. There had been a history of interracial strife in the area. Earlier, an Hispanic police officer had shot two African-American men, sparking riots. The atmosphere had just begun to stabilize when Ike was killed, and the detective feared that racial riots would reignite. Generally, blacks had been hostile toward the police in the past, but now the African-American community was contacting the police, trying to give information that could help solve the case. The detective on the case said that he had never seen such community involvement and cooperation. This had never happened in Miami, and the police felt a new sense of confidence in society. When the detective flew to Lancaster several days later, he repeated the story to the Lancaster police officers. This was the second sign to me that God was in control.

One day I picked up Ike's Bible, and it fell open to some notes from a Sunday school class he had taught the week before. He had asked each member to think of an experience they had gone through when God was especially close to them, and then think of a way to share that with others. The notes were like a personal message for me and our children. Throughout this incredible experience I felt that God was so near, providing strength, calmness, and peace in an overwhelming way. I wanted to be able to share how this affected my life.

The funeral director informed me that he couldn't repair the damage to Ike's head adequately enough to have a viewing, but he could arrange for the family to view him if we wished. I didn't want to see my husband again. I had blocked the image of the shooting from my mind and was afraid that seeing him again would reinforce that picture. I told the children to choose whether they wanted to see him or not, and they also chose against it.

However, our daughter Dawn, who lives in New York, had some doubts about the decision. She didn't get home often and was afraid that if she didn't see his body, she might not accept that he was gone. Just as we were talking the telephone rang. It was a woman whom I had never met, but she said I had been on her mind and she wanted to call. Twenty years earlier she, too, had lost her husband to the gunshot of a robber. She wanted to see his body later but was not allowed to, and now she was thankful that she could remember him as he was. I related the phone call to Dawn, and she decided not to see the body. I was grateful for the timing of the phone call. It couldn't have been a coincidence.

Ike's funeral was held on Sunday, December 17, a frigid and snow-covered day. Hundreds of people filled the New Holland Mennonite Church, surrounding our family and sharing the pain. The words of the hymns gave me hope and confidence as they resounded through the building, ". . . the body they may kill, God's truth abideth still . . . "

Many persons contributed to make the day easier for the children and me. A friend took care of my grandson, others dealt with the news media, and our pastor prepared a comforting sermon. Somebody recorded the service, and another friend made copies of the tape at no charge to us, so we could share the service with those who couldn't attend. I didn't have to worry about who would usher or park the cars. Everything was taken care of.

One night I had a dream that the men who murdered Ike were outside my house, trying to break in. I awoke with a jolt, paralyzed with fear, my heart pounding. After that, several friends committed themselves to praying that I would never be tortured again with bad dreams or flashbacks. I haven't experienced another dream or flashback since.

The flood of cards and letters continued long after the funeral. People wrote who didn't know us, to assure us that they cared. I was comforted by letters from people who had been through similar tragedies. They offered me wisdom from their experiences and assured me that God would be with me through the lonely days ahead. Florida residents wrote, expressing their sorrow that our visit to their state had ended so tragically. A little bit of pain was eased with every letter that arrived, and we were overwhelmed by the love and thoughtfulness of both our friends and strangers.

Sharing also came in the form of financial aid. The first gift came from a shipping company who sent the bus to Costa Rica free of charge. We had already paid the shipping bill, and the company refunded the full $1800 to the Costa Rican church. My daughter and son-in-law were given free plane tickets to fly from Costa Rica for the funeral, and large contributions were made for a much needed building for their church.

On the home front, I had hired the services of a lawyer to iron out legalities, and he insisted on offering his services free of charge. A neighbor and his friend (whom I didn't know) spent hours putting new plumbing in our basement. In the spring I discovered the house roof was in poor repair, so on Good Friday weekend 30 friends, relatives, and members of my church family spent two days replacing it and doing other maintenance jobs. A water problem in the basement also appeared with the spring thaw, and the masonry company my son works for waterproofed it at minimal cost to me.

Over the six months that followed Ike's death, I felt the presence of God's people around me constantly. Rarely a day passed without visitors and calls. Two or three times a week I was invited to eat with friends and family.

It was time to pick up the pieces of my life and put them back together. I had already cleaned out Ike's drawers and closet so I could distribute his belongings among the children before they returned to their homes. One day I came across an old pair of his shoes. They were torn and dirty from being worn when Ike mowed the lawn or repaired a car. My first instinct was, "No one will want these; I'll throw them away." But at that moment, the finality and reality of Ike's death hit me with a surge of pain, as though I had just tried to throw some part of myself away. I learned the meaning of pain and suffering in those months, as I had never known before. However, I also learned the depth behind the verses, "I will never leave you or forsake you" and "God is my refuge and my strength, a very present help in trouble." I had repeated those verses for years, but often they were little more than words. Now they were filled with such potency that I felt they were written for me.

I've been told, "Ike was a gentle man. It's not right that he should have died like that." The fact remains that Christians suffer the same things others suffer. But there is a difference. Even though God didn't explain the reasons for this event in my life, I know that in every circumstance God will be there to comfort me. He sent others to hold me until I could stand again. When Ike died, my life felt so completely out of control that I was forced to rely entirely on God. When I let go of my own resources,

I found peace in the midst of pain and grief and experienced a closeness to God's love like never before. It was then that I realized how much we need each other, and how dependent we are on the love, prayers, and support of fellow Christians. In the face of a traumatic situation, we forget disagreements and drop our masks. Making a good impression was of no concern to me, and I was able to relate to others in a deeply genuine way. That, in turn, helped to generate a deep love and appreciation for others within me.

C.S. Lewis calls pain God's megaphone. He wrote that God whispers to us in our joy; God speaks to us in our conscience; God shouts to us in our pain.

Suffering and death made me stop and listen to what God had to say. I have heard God say, through the Bible and through people, "I love you." Suffering isn't unique to me. All of us suffer in our lifetimes. No two people go through the same thing, but God remains faithful.

Who will separate us from the love of Christ? Shall trouble or hardship or persecution or famine or nakedness or danger or sword? No, in all these things we are more than conquerors through him who loved us. For I am convinced that neither death nor life, neither angels nor demons, neither the present nor the future, nor any powers, neither height nor depth, nor anything else in all creation, will be able to separate us from the love of God that is in Jesus Christ our Lord.
—Romans 8: 35, 37-38, NIV

I don't know why God allowed death for Ike and life for me. But God has been faithful to both of us. Ike is in heaven, enjoying the eternal life with God that he looked forward to for over 40 years. God didn't allow me to enter this difficult situation alone. Every step of the way I have been carried when I am too weak and helpless to walk on my own. God continues to surround me with love—both his own and the love of his people.

I am Chippewa and attend the Strawberry Lake Mennonite Church in Ogema, Minnesota. Within the span of a year and a half, my mother, father, and grandmother died. I felt confident that I could handle this. However, the loss was too great for me to withstand. I am so glad that God intervened through the loving care of my husband who suggested that I go back to school. This would help me keep my mind on other things. Yes, it did take my mind off my great loss.

Throughout my college experience the presence of God was real to me. I could visualize his hand taking mine and guiding my way. God opened the doors. My classes were flexible to meet my needs.

I studied to be a teacher and now teach at the Circle of Life School on the White Earth Reservation. God provided a love in me to help my students with their struggles. I give them hugs and tell them that I care. I have more patience toward my students when difficult situations arise, and then get a smile, hug, or "I love you, Teacher." This reminds me of God's care and I am thankful.

Lola Dodd
Ogema, Minnesota

UPROOTED
By Divorce

When his wife Mim filed for divorce, Carl Swartz felt like his world was falling apart. All his life he had believed that divorce was sinful and wrong. Now he was in a completely contradictory position to that conviction.

For five years before Mim filed for divorce, their marriage had deteriorated to a point that they communicated little. But Carl was blind to the emotional separation that had already occurred between them. Though he had no thoughts of ending the marriage, Carl now realized that he had made only a meager attempt to improve his relationship with his wife. When Mim walked out on the marriage, Carl had to deal not only with his grief, but also with his attitude toward divorce.

"I never tried to understand what divorced people went through. I was quick to judge them. I didn't know or understand the pain involved in a marital breakup, or the need for supportive people until I lived through it myself.

"Throughout our marriage, Mim and I attended a small Mennonite church. We liked the congregation. The members were a mix of professionals and laborers. Since many of our social activities were church-related, our separation touched many of the church members."

Both Mim and Carl continued to attend the church after they were separated, which created some awkwardness for them. Carl did feel cared for by the congregation. He admits he was treated more compassionately than he had treated other people in similar circumstances in years past. When local newspapers printed the news of Carl's and Mim's separation, their pastor called Carl to ask whether he could include them in his prayer the following Sunday. Carl agreed.

"After beginning to pray, the pastor was overcome with

emotion and couldn't finish. Others in the congregation also shed tears, and it was apparent to me that they were grieving with Mim and me. I now felt that I would not need to tackle the pain of separation alone. I experienced the reality of the verse that says, 'When one member of the body of Christ suffers, all members suffer.' "

The separation between Mim and Carl grew hostile. The court eventually intervened, and Carl was awarded custody of their three children.

Soon afterward Carl met a woman named Pam, and they began to see each other on a regular basis. The church that had grieved with and supported Carl in the early stages of separation had difficulty accepting his choice to begin a dating relationship. Carl realizes that the timing of his relationship with Pam may have been poor judgment. The divorce was not final. When the church heard that he was dating someone while he was still married to Mim, some of the members began to pull away from him.

"I had told Pam from the start that church was an essential part of my life. She was anxious to go to my church, and agreed to attend with me on Easter Sunday. However, when one of the elders heard of our plans, he called me early on Good Friday to discourage me from bringing Pam to church."

When Carl told Pam, she was deeply hurt. Friends she worked with thought it was ludicrous for a church not to welcome someone, and they encouraged her to go anyway. She invited her sister to go with her and the two of them arrived together on Sunday morning.

"Pam and her sister sat with me in the back of the church feeling very alone and unwelcome. That ended Pam's desire to associate with my church. And, for the first time, I felt like an outsider among people I had known intimately for 20 years. "

Only a few people from the congregation kept in contact with Carl after that. He received a letter from one couple saying that they missed him. Another couple invited Pam and him to their home for a meal. These acts of kindness meant a great deal to Carl.

"In the past I looked to the church for help when I was in

difficult situations. Now, when I needed the church most, it was simply not there. The fact that I had lost both my marriage and my church family greatly intensified my sense of loss."

Carl went on an emotional roller coaster during the divorce proceedings. The church supplied a mediator to help Carl and Mim with the settlement and division of their property. But things remained strained and tense between them. Carl lost much personal property and suffered huge financial losses in the settlement. It was even more painful to lose one daughter to Mim in the child custody battle.

When the divorce was finalized, Carl and Pam were married. "We got married with what looked like more problems than Mim and I faced when we began our marriage. But Pam and I have grown together in our relationship. We love each other deeply and share every area of our lives with each other. The church we now attend (not Mennonite) has been warm and receptive, and has further enriched our marriage.

"My journey has been incredibly painful. Many parts of my life shattered along with my marriage, and it has been difficult to put my roots down in another church. I am not bitter toward the church. I am still a Mennonite at heart. My hope is that someday Pam and I can be involved in a Mennonite church."

Two days before open heart surgery, Dick Walter had a dream "that a whole bunch of Mennonites were praying for me." The dream was a special gift to Dick and his wife, Beulah. She said, "It made me feel good! That's the way it was. There were people all over praying."

Because of Dick's job, the Walters no longer live in a Mennonite community. However, they still feel very much connected to the Mennonite church. When they became aware that Dick would need surgery, Beulah called both of the Mennonite churches they used to attend, and these congregations gladly committed themselves to prayer. Several days following surgery when Beulah was particularly discouraged, she thought, "Well, why not call them again?" She did. And they prayed.

Dick received dozens of cards, calls, flowers, and letters from persons he had not been in touch with for years. "What surprises me," Dick said, "is the long memory of the Mennonites. It's wonderful!"

Dick greatly appreciated the effort that friends made to visit him. "One friend drove 300 miles from Allentown and back that same day." One evening two friends from Cleveland drove to his hospital bed, visited him for a few minutes, and then drove back again.

Dick experienced several bad post-surgery hallucinations. He said, "I am sure that the prayers of the saints really undergirded me." A verse that was especially helpful to him during this time was sent by a friend: " 'Because he loves me,' says the Lord, 'I will rescue him; I will protect him, for he acknowledges my name' " (Psalm 91:14).

Dick and Beulah Walter
Pittsburgh, Pennsyvlania

BETWEEN
LİFE ANd DEATH

"It had been a routine day," Joyce reflected. "After a full day of work, we had a relaxing time of lap swimming and were getting ready for bed. We were rather silly, as we often are, and Phil jokingly said, 'Okay, nurse, tell me why this side of my abdomen is hard and the other side is soft.' I felt it, and I immediately knew something was drastically wrong. But, since we were in a joking mood, I said, 'Oh, I think you are going to have a baby.' That baby turned out to be a very enlarged spleen. By the following morning the word 'leukemia' was ringing in our ears. We had never anticipated working with such an illness."

"We live in the small town of Hesston, Kansas, with a very effective grapevine," Phil observed, "and, in no time at all, the community knew we were facing a major crisis."

On the following Sunday morning, Joyce and Phil Bedsworth described their growing concerns with the congregation of Hesston Mennonite Church, where Phil served as pastor. There were "significant shadows on the horizon," Phil said, "and it was a journey we wanted them to take with us. There were many teary eyes that morning, and a very swift response."

The original prognosis for this particular kind of leukemia offered Phil a life expectancy of three to five years. Within the first month the Bedsworths explored possibilities for Phil to have a bone marrow transplant. A successful transplant required the bone marrow of a sibling, whose marrow would first need to be tested to discover if it matched Phil's. His only sister agreed to have her marrow checked, and, although the match was not perfect, it was adequate to proceed with the surgery.

At the time, Joyce was enrolled in a medical ethics class that raised serious questions about the worth of a single life. The risks and expense of the bone marrow transplant were overwhelming, and it was disheartening to realize that the amount of money needed for Phil's transplant could furnish hundreds of lower income families with prenatal service. So what right did they have to spend such a large sum of money on one life?

The weight of ethical questions, in addition to the imminence of Phil's medical needs, was more than the Bedsworths could digest. Phil and Joyce included their church family in discerning a method of treatment. They prepared a fact sheet about the costs of the bone marrow surgery and approached the congregation with an appeal for guidance.

"They worked very hard with us," Phil said, "and we sensed their loving concern. But at the same time, we sensed their frustration in knowing whether to counsel us to simply let me die as comfortably as possible or take heroic measures to extend my life. We were asking a very personal question about stewardship of medical and financial resources."

Both Phil and Joyce felt a strong need to address the possibility of death and make the necessary preparations for the dying process. They knew this was plausible for Phil, but their son Steven, who suffered from chronic severe asthma, was also at risk of death.

"We went to a Holiday Inn one weekend and wrote our funeral plans. I did not want to be alone in making funeral arrangements for any member of the family, so we made funeral plans for ourselves and for our children," Joyce recalled.

"We looked at our finances and the titling of our cars and house. We wrote letters to the children for their eighth grade and high school graduations and for their wedding days. We wrote tributes to each other and tributes to each child."

The decision process between Phil and Joyce and the congregation moved slowly until the original diagnosis was discovered to be an error. The revised prognosis gave Phil three to five months of life rather than three to five years. If they were to proceed with a transplant, it would need to be done very quickly.

"We felt that we needed additional support beyond that which the congregation could provide," Phil said, "so we called together a small support group of four couples. This group helped us in making critical decisions and coordinated every important detail in our lives when we were unable to. We chose Iowa City as the location for treatment, because the University of Iowa Hospital offered excellent medical care and there was a community of Mennonite churches nearby.

Although the decision provided some sense of relief, there also came the complexities of establishing care for their children and housing for Joyce during Phil's recovery in Iowa City. Both friends and strangers emerged to offer their service during this time.

"We arranged for a support member to have check-writing privileges on our accounts. Our associate pastor and his wife agreed to be surrogate Mom and Dad to our children, and they moved into our house. Many people helped with meals and cleaning. Steven's health was a frightening thing, so we trained a group of 18 people to help with his nighttime care in the event of his illness."

In Iowa City, a couple from a local Mennonite church, who did not know the Bedsworths, opened their home to Joyce. Phil would need a recovery time of two months to a year after the transplant, and this family took Joyce in as a daughter, providing housing, meals, and emotional support through the duration of Phil's treatment.

Phil's primary physician, Dr. Roger Gingrich, was also a member of the Iowa City Mennonite Church. It was comforting to share common beliefs and values with him, after their previous struggles with ethical questions. This provided the base for a highly significant patient/doctor relationship.

"Joyce and I moved to Iowa City in January of 1987, and I had the bone marrow transplant. I went through six hours of total body radiation and massive chemotherapy to destroy my own immune system so that I could receive a new one. Much of that time I was in isolation. However, we did not feel cut off from the church. Each mail time we would get from 10 to 20 remembrances. Somehow the "Menno-vine" had spread our story across the country. We got letters from Ohio, Indiana, Pennsylvania, Virginia, Alabama, and elsewhere. Many of these people did not know us, but when they heard that a family within the Mennonite fellowship was going through a very difficult time, they wanted to lend their support.

"Mail time became a high point for us. I had a pentagon-shaped room, and we began a ritual of putting the cards on the wall as we received them. By the time I was dismissed, four of the five walls were covered with cards, notes, and letters."

Phil was able to return to Hesston in February of 1987, almost two months after the transplant." I had promised the congregation that I would be back to preach on Easter, and my first Sunday back was Easter Sunday. One of the images that had become special to us during my illness was that of a cocoon and caterpillar transforming into a butterfly. As a way of illustrating this, I went to the church early that day, and situated myself on the platform, covered with a big bed sheet. During children's time, the children were told about caterpillars and butterflies. They were then invited to clap or yell or call my name. When they did, I threw off the blanket and emerged from my 'cocoon.' (Because of chemotherapy, I had lost my hair and was wearing a wig. I was a little concerned that my wig might fall off, but I managed to keep it on). I then preached my Easter sermon."

"Before we went for the bone marrow transplant, we had purchased 1,000 gladiola bulbs," Joyce noted. "We chose the gladiola because it was a symbol of our wedding day. On Easter Sunday we distributed bulbs to everyone. This act symbolized our gratitude for Phil's life and our hope for continuing life."

"By summer I was able to team up again with the church staff," Phil added. "Things looked encouraging. We thought we had come out winners through a very difficult time."

The spirit of their church family carried Phil and Joyce through the rough waters of the transplant, but their lives still teetered precariously on the edge of a seemingly bottomless gorge. In October, Phil began to experience kidney failure as a result of his bone marrow treatment. An infection triggered total kidney failure, resulting in six months of dialysis. This proved to be the most difficult experience of their lives, straining their relationship with the congregation.

"One result of losing kidney function is to lose emotion. I didn't feel happy, sad, or angry. I couldn't concentrate. I couldn't remember. I dragged myself from one dialysis treatment to another. For me, life was very much a blur. It was a difficult time for Joyce as well. She felt there was some detachment by members of the church."

"But," Joyce added, "I am not blaming the church. It was a time when I was not able to really state my needs. People were always willing to do what I asked of them. Even so, I felt increasingly isolated. People just didn't know what to say or do. And we weren't a very pleasant family to be around."

"Not only was it a difficult time for us, it was a difficult time for the congregation also," Phil noted. "Generally, as a church we do a fantastic job when acute care is needed. During hospitalization or death, we rally by bringing in casseroles and by providing child care. But chronic care has its own special demands. The needs of the sick continue, day after day, with little or no sign of progress. The problem never goes away. Care-givers are continually reminded of their own mortality. Sometimes they find the task simply too overwhelming and frightening, and they need to pull back out of sheer exhaustion."

Six months of dialysis left Phil with a dismal outlook. Discontinuing treatment would have essentially meant pulling the plug on his life. His name was among 10,000 others on a waiting list for a kidney transplant, but with his past medical history, it was unlikely that he would qualify. For a kidney transplant to be successful, the donor and the recipient must have two out of six medical match points in common. With each additional matching point, there is an increased likelihood of success.

Their small group continued to provide strength, and they held an anointing service for Phil on June 29, 1988. Phil recalls, "Within 48 hours, we received a call from Iowa City, telling us that an 18-year-old man from Texas had been killed in a car accident, and that his kidney and mine were a perfect six-point match. Our support group immediately kicked into action, and, by 7:30 the next morning, Joyce and I were on a plane owned by one of our church members, flying to Iowa City.

"By 9:00 p.m., I was in surgery. Throughout that time, churches in Hesston and across the land were remembering us in prayer. The doctors had very candidly told us that, with my history, I might never get off the operating table. But I did, and within a month I was able to return to Hesston and start the rebuilding process once more."

Once again, new life streamed through Phil's veins and his spirits lifted. But in October, a side effect of Phil's medication caused cataracts in both of his eyes, and he was unable to drive. The church continued to present solutions—a dozen or more senior citizens volunteered to accompany Phil on pastoral visits to sick and elderly church members. There were many opportunities for conversation between visits, and Phil found the interaction to be enriching.

"Often they would accompany me into the hospital rooms, and their additional presence was a great blessing. When I could drive again, I almost hesitated to do so because of the rich experience it had been to work alongside the older people."

Throughout his illness, Phil remained in the pastoral position at Hesston Mennonite Church. His health was stabilizing, and it seemed natural for him to continue. However, a new shadow emerged when another side effect appeared from previous medications. Malignant tumors were spreading rapidly in both lungs, and his right lung collapsed before treatment was initiated. The cancer's siege brought Phil very close to death, and again they sought high risk treatment in Iowa City.

"This was another of the more difficult moments for us. The Hesston congregation had walked with us through our mountains and valleys, and this roller coaster had made them very tired. With so many uncertainties about my future health, Joyce and I, through mutual agreement with the congregation, decided that I would complete my pastoral term in the summer of 1989."

The Bedsworth family has endured their share of trials, and the future is unpredictable. In spite of this, they do not harbor bitterness toward God for the pain they have suffered. Phil has looked for answers in the midst of the adversity, but has avoided blaming God.

"Did God strike me down? No. God doesn't go around zapping people. But neither does God exempt us from suffering. One of our learnings through this whole experience is that there is a difference between healing and curing. Joyce and I both desire that I be cured. We have a strong marriage of 17 years, and we would like to add another 50 to it. I'd like to see the kids graduate from high school, and I would like to share in their wedding days. But neither of these is highly likely. Many things in life simply can't be fixed or cured, but we are learning that healing is always possible.

"As I think back through our experiences, and especially those with our local congregation," Phil reflected, "I am deeply grateful. The whole process has transformed Hesston for us. Both Joyce and I are from the eastern part of the United States, and during our first few years at Hesston it was simply a place to live. Now, because of the church reaching out to us, it has become our home.

"We remind ourselves that there are ways to celebrate in the midst of the difficult situations. Several times during hospitalization we wrote pastoral epistles to the congregation. I think I have a better appreciation for how the Apostle Paul might have felt in being away from the sisters and brothers in Christ whom he loved so much. As with Paul, we tried to communicate our care and concern for people of our congregation."

"I've marveled at how people have given of themselves in caring for us in so many ways," Joyce added. "One night when Phil was in intensive care, and it seemed that life could be snatched away at any time, I came home from the hospital feeling discouraged and very vulnerable. But upon my return I discovered a bouquet of gorgeous red tulips on the table. They became for me a vision of renewed hope.

"With each of Phil's sick spells, our children always ask the question, 'Could Daddy die?' And our answer is always, 'Yes.' We have tried to be open and honest with them. Whenever we flew to Iowa City, Phil told the children good-bye, meaning that we didn't know if Daddy would ever come home again. We have been deeply touched by how people have walked with us through these hard times of saying good-bye.

"In these past years, the image that I have is of God picking us up—the four of us—and holding us in his hand, surrounded and supported by his people. We haven't walked this journey on our own. We've been carried through by God's people."

"We have a sense of peace and confidence that we are not alone, that there is meaning in life in the midst of suffering. We are seeing more clearly that death is God's final act of grace, bringing rest and resolution to life's pains and struggles."

Phil died on March 18, 1993 in Wichita, Kansas, at the age of 42. He had been hospitalized since he suffered a heart attack on March 9. He and Joyce wrote a more complete story of their struggles with Phil's illness in Fight the Good Fight, *published by Herald Press.*

Nick Roth was baptized as a young man, but then dropped out of the church, a separation that lasted for well over 50 years. Several years ago I learned to know him and discovered we had a mutual interest in woodworking. His wife attended the church where I am pastor, and for years many people in the congregation had prayed that Nick would come back to Christ and into the church. I made numerous contacts with him. If I needed a tool or some advice, I went out of my way to ask him. He was always happy to help me or lend me what I needed. We established a good rapport with each other and I found him to be a very tender man.

The only time he came to the church was for funerals. Many times I observed him cry and it appeared to me that he was under some sort of conviction, but just couldn't make a commitment. I visited him occasionally, and tried to lead him back into a relationship with Christ and God. I believe he really wanted to, but it was very difficult for him to actually do it.

Recently he called me late on a Saturday night. He was very sick and he asked me to come. He wanted to make a commitment to the Lord and prayed confessionally with me. He broke down and cried, confessing his sins and asking Jesus to come into his life. It is taking time for him to get into the flow of the congregation again, but he rejoined the church on May 16, 1993 at the age of 78.

Lloyd Gingerich
Milford, Nebraska

CONTINUING
THE CYCLE

As a young boy in Tuxpan, a small village in the Guerrero province of Mexico, Sam Lopez dreamed of a life in the United States. His parents had left Sam and his siblings in the care of his grandparents while they attempted to better their lives in Chicago. When they could, they would send money to have their children join them. Now, years later, Sam lives in a small town in Pennsylvania. His trek there was beyond the scope of his childish imaginings.

Sam was a teenager when he left Mexico with his sisters and brothers to join their parents in Illinois. To their dismay, their parents were separated and planning to divorce. Sam was angry and rebellious. His aunt offered him and his siblings some stability throughout their transition, and invited them to go to church with her. At that time Sam's only contact with religion was through his grandfather's storytelling. The Bible stories he told had little effect on Sam, however. He didn't believe or understand them. He told his aunt he had no interest in going to church, but his three sisters began to attend the Spanish Mennonite Church on a regular basis. They eventually persuaded Sam to go with them.

"It was there that I saw something was missing in my life," Sam recalls. It was through the Spanish Mennonite Church in Chicago that a seed was planted within him. The congregation encouraged his desire to learn and offered him financial help to attend a Nazarene seminary in Texas. When he heard a Mennonite theologian, J.C. Wenger, speak at the seminary, he realized how little he knew of Mennonite beliefs. Unlike other speakers, Wenger mingled with the students and entered into discussions with them. "I realized I was a Mennonite at heart, even though I didn't know what a Mennonite was," says Sam. "I wanted to learn about the Mennonite beliefs. J.C. Wenger's behavior indicated that there was something different about Mennonites."

After Sam graduated, he married Soledad Martinez, and they moved to Indiana to attend a Mennonite college. Sam completed a degree at Goshen College in 1980. Leaders of the Spanish churches asked him to be a pastor, but Sam first wanted to complete seminary studies in a Mennonite seminary.

But finances were a roadblock to his further education. There was little food in the refrigerator, and Sam didn't have the money for groceries, let alone ten extra dollars to use for the registration fee to Goshen Biblical Seminary.

"By God's grace, I received $10 in the mail from a sister from the Spanish Mennonite congregation in Chicago. I decided to use the money for eggs, milk, and bread. On the way to the store I saw the seminary application on the car seat. Instead of the supermarket, I drove to Goshen Biblical Seminary and went to the admissions office for an interview. They asked me how much money I had to study at the seminary. I said I had only the $10 application fee. The financial aid counselor listened to me. I told them about my life and why I wanted to study in a Mennonite seminary. The admissions counselor asked me to wait outside his office for a few minutes. In less than five minutes he called me in and said, 'Here is a $700 check for you. Your books and studies are paid.' The Spanish Mennonite Church in Goshen offered aid so I could attend seminary. They believed in me, and helped with my formation as a Christian and a Mennonite. Through their kindness and love I felt God saying, 'I am providing you with everything.'

"After I graduated from seminary, my wife and I went to Oregon where her father was the pastor of a Mennonite congregation. The small church of 25 to 30 people knew I had studied at the seminary and were very supportive of us. They helped us with financial aid because I couldn't find work and offered their spiritual support and prayer.

"I was without work for almost six months. At the same time, I didn't know if I wanted to be a missionary or a preacher. I just trusted in God to show me where to go. Now I see that trust was faith, but at that time I didn't know what it was."

While praying in December, 1983, Sam felt God was asking him to go to Pennsylvania. He had never been to Pennsylvania before, but felt he should take the calling seriously. "I talked with a group of about 25 people from the church in Oregon and asked them to pray with me and tell me whether they also sensed I should go. All of them affirmed the calling. My wife and her father also felt at peace with it. If our church community had objected and felt we should not move, I don't think we would have."

Sam knew only one person in Pennsylvania. José Santiago was a Mennonite bishop whom he had met once during seminary. He called José and told him about his prayer and his sense of God's calling him to Pennsylvania. "If you feel God calling you, you should come," José told him.

"We left Oregon with $250 dollars for food and gas. It was winter. My wife was expecting a baby, and we were traveling with our two small children. We had no place to stay, no work, and no insurance for my wife to have the child. Still, she and I felt that we must go there. We went to Chicago and stayed with my family for Christmas before continuing on to New Holland, Pennsylvania.

"When we arrived in Pennsylvania we went to José's house, and, because he had family staying with him, he made arrangements for us to stay in the New Holland Spanish Mennonite Church building. The congregation agreed to give us shelter in an upstairs room. They moved aside tables and chairs and put a bed there. They opened their arms even though they never met us, and said we could stay in the church for a couple of months. José came every day to take us to eat at his house, or another brother or sister from the congregation would invite us for a meal.

"I'm grateful that God guided me to this congregation. I have learned a lot from their act of sharing with my family. In return, I shared my teaching abilities with them. People learned to know me, not just as the man whom they helped, but as a friend, brother, and teacher. Once, while I was leading a Bible study, one of the leaders in the church began to cry and asked my forgiveness. He said he hadn't agreed with the church for giving my family housing and food. He explained that he misjudged me for bringing my family from Oregon. I was touched that he was open to confessing."

In mid-January Sam found work in a local poultry operation. His health benefits would not become effective until late March, and their baby was due in the beginning of March. He knew they could not afford to pay the medical costs of delivery, and prayed the baby would be born later.

Sam was overjoyed when the baby arrived, healthy and whole. He looked down at the small arm and read the date of birth on the hospital bracelet: March 25, 1984. This was the exact day his coverage went into effect! Sam wept, and told the nurse, "This is March 25!" Sam remarked, "She was completely puzzled as to why I was so excited about March 25! But that day, I knew God heard my prayer.

"In six months I was Assistant Pastor of this church. They helped us find an apartment, and the church paid our rent. This congregation helped me a lot, both with shelter and with my spiritual growth and development."

New Holland Spanish Mennonite Church is composed of people from South and Central Americas and the Caribbean. When Sam arrived, the members of the church were mostly Puerto Rican and Colombian. He became aware of some feelings of rivalry between the two nationalities. "Now their theology is changing. The congregation is beginning to understand the Kingdom of God is not only for one nation, but all nations. One challenge we face is how we, as a Mennonite church, help all people without any prejudice or racism. Not only should we help people we like, but also those who we have reservations about. The love of God can overcome all of our differences, but we must be willing to obey. We need to show that we are a different kind of people."

Each year there is a fair in the town of New Holland; the Spanish Mennonite Church charges two dollars for people to use their parking lot. Several years ago, two young Mexican men arrived in New Holland during the fair. They began to talk with Sam, and he invited them to come to church on Sunday. "They had no vision for the future and had wandered state to state," he remembers. "We made them feel welcome and they found friends among us. We helped them financially and gave them clothing. They were invited into our homes to eat. We wanted to help them as a sign of God's love for them and to show that our belief in Christ called us to respond to their needs."

Both of the young men were baptized in the church and are now working in New Holland and participating in the congregation. "When I told them the story of how I came here and was also helped by the church," Sam says, "they were amazed. I was like them. I had nothing, and the congregation helped me. Later, when I was able, I helped these young men, who are now capable of giving to others. Sharing is a cycle."

For Sam, the cycle has led him to become pastor of the New Holland church and, eventually, Director of the Spanish Bible Institute in New Holland. He is active in the Spanish Mennonite Council of Churches and has served as President of the Spanish Mennonite Convention for the U.S. and Canada.

"I asked one of the young men why he came to accept God, and he said, 'Because I felt the love of God among you.' He started to see that there was a mission here and wanted to be a part of that. I've seen both of them help others to find purpose and vision for their lives. That is a story I am grateful to be part of. I recognize God's hand and grace in these things."

How many women would admit to feeling butterflies at the sound of their husband's voice on the phone after 30 years of marriage? Mary and Ron Dearing had that sort of relationship. At age 50, their business was paid for and doing well. All of their children were married and starting families. Life couldn't be much better than this.

When Mary noticed a lump developing in her breast, they both worried. The diagnosis confirmed their fears and she went through a radical mastectomy, followed by radiation and chemotherapy. With a $5,000 deductible from Mennonite Mutual Aid Plan, their expenses were substantial. Our little church, with a $13,000 annual budget, gave Mary and Ron a $1,000 love offering. They accepted it gratefully, but later returned it to the church to be used for a special project.

At a later time, the congregation offered them catastrophe aid. They expressed their thanks, but were certain someone else needed the money more than they did.

After five years of treatment, Mary's doctor declared her cancer arrested. About that time, Ron developed symptoms; his disease was considered inoperable and deadly. He was diagnosed to live less than a year.

After receiving a second opinion, Ron accepted his illness and set about to prepare his family for his death. Before he died, he taught Mary how to run the business, explaining how to sell steel to contractors and run the fabrication and welding shop. She learned quickly and today her reputation is known in 17 counties throughout southern Ohio. When asked the secret of his success Ron would answer, "I just follow the Golden Rule."

Today Mary serves as Treasurer of Hillside Mennonite Chapel. She occasionally looks back on her hardships and wonders why it all happened. One thing I know—she has shown many people how a Christian woman faces cancer and wins for the glory of God.

Jim Mullett
Jackson, Ohio

Rape:
New Territory

It was a usual sort of Monday in November when the Nafziger family, Rodney, Miriam, and their three-year-old daughter, Rachel, gathered for supper. Afterward, Rodney left their home on the campus of Associated Mennonite Biblical Seminaries in Elkhart, Indiana, to study at the library. Miriam took Rachel on several errands at a nearby shopping center.

Returning home, she prepared Rachel for bed and read stories to her in Rodney and Miriam's bedroom. She knew Rodney would be home soon, so, as usual, she left the kitchen door unlocked and one light on. By 9:30, Rachel was asleep. As Miriam carried her back to her bedroom, she heard the door open and Rodney's footsteps approaching. The man who appeared in the bedroom doorway, however, was not Rodney, but a stranger masked by several layers of women's hosiery. Miriam stood up and turned on the light. "What are you doing here?" she asked angrily. She was keenly aware of Rachel, sleeping in the bed beside her.

Things happened very quickly. With his hand over her mouth, the intruder pulled Miriam to the floor, ordering her not to scream. Rachel awoke, startled and wide-eyed.

The man forced Miriam to her feet and pushed her into the living room. Fearing that he might hurt Rachel, she gave little resistance. Somehow Miriam remained calm enough to engage the man in conversation as he laid her on the floor and molested her. Her fear and anxiety turned into chatter. Was he married? No. Did he study? No. The personal questions she asked seemed to make him lose his confidence. She speculated that she might know this man, perhaps as a student at the Seminary. He fondled and molested her, but told her he did not intend to have intercourse. When he pushed up his mask to kiss her she felt coarse facial hair brush against her face, but she couldn't distinguish other facial features in the darkened room.

She continued to say, "You must be struggling with a lot of problems." He admitted, that, yes, he had many problems. Miriam told him she was a daughter of Jesus Christ, the whole time praying that Rodney would come home. She asked if she could help him find counseling. The man finally said he would leave if she promised to tell no one. "We are going to pray for you," she said. "Tell me your name. I know you won't give me your real name, but if I have a name I can pray for you."

"It's Tim." He paused, and then ran out of the house. Rodney arrived home at 9:45.

A neighboring Seminary professor, whom Rodney talked with the night of the rape, connected the Nafzigers with a counselor the following day. They are thankful for that connection, because in their post-trauma state they might not have had the emotional strength to contact help on their own.

The counselor, who taught some classes at the Seminary, helped guide Miriam and Rodney through recovery. He told them that it would probably take two years for Miriam to get over the rape. "I found that hard to believe," Miriam recalls. "I remember thinking 'Two years? I'm going to start processing right now!' I learned quickly that it just takes time."

In addition to their own needs, they came to him with concern for their daughter. Miriam had asked the policeman who investigated the rape whether he thought Rachel would need therapy after witnessing the assault. He insisted that a three-year-old child was too young to be affected. The counselor, however, confirmed Miriam's suspicions that Rachel's trauma needed to be acknowledged. He showed Miriam and Rodney several types of exercises to use with Rachel and told them how to explain the assault in terms she would understand.

Rodney and Miriam practiced the play therapy with their daughter. They assumed that someone would refer them to a child therapist, but no one ever did. Miriam recognizes now that her mind was too self-focused and muddled to meet her daughter's needs. "In processing the incident eight years later," Miriam says, "we've felt inadequate in handling Rachel's needs.

However, we've tried to counteract that inadequacy by talking with her about her memories. She's old enough now to clarify her feelings, and she has been very candid with us."

Rachel, as a 12-year-old, remembers certain specifics about the frightening event and has been frank about her memories and feelings. She has told her parents that a therapist would have been helpful, because, while Rodney and Miriam had a counselor to go to for advice, she had only them for comfort and help. The memory of Rachel's unmet needs brings forth the most pain and emotion for Miriam and Rodney. In hindsight the Nafzigers wish that a friend or other outsider could have helped them be more objective in supporting Rachel during the days that followed the rape. At that point they were incapable.

News of the rape shocked family and friends alike. The Nafzigers found themselves on a new frontier in the Mennonite church. No one they knew had ever experienced rape or even known someone who had been assaulted in this way.

At times Miriam stumbled blindly through the steps of sharing her story, unsure of what response would follow. "In the beginning, retelling my story was a significant phase of recovery. Each time I reviewed the incident, I explored a different corner of it. There is no way any one person can stand to listen to the story as many times as a victim needs to tell it. However, I began to realize that there were some persons I could talk to and others whom I couldn't. Sometimes I would tell the story to someone and end up having to counsel them because they felt so badly about it. Our friends had no experience responding to my particular needs as a victim of rape. Still, when we started telling others, it became another step of healing for me, and I am thankful to all the people who listened."

Small clusters of people from the Seminary were the most effective in offering Miriam and Rodney support and listening ears. "The church we attended wasn't sure how to respond to me in relation to the rape. Although I shared in a small group setting, Rodney and I gravitated to the Seminary community for understanding and counsel. I needed to find people in the church and Seminary who would not try to solve things too quickly, but would just journey with me."

Grace and reassurance came from friends and strangers. Miriam sought out listeners in the church. Several days after the crisis she told a co-worker who also attended her church. He continued to be a supportive friend and listener throughout the following months. Rodney was able to express his pain to a small group of Seminary students. Though he felt a sense of support, he generally found it difficult for other men to understand why he was unsettled by the rape since he was not the victim. Many of his professors, however, were sensitive to Rodney's needs. They offered him extensions on papers and projects which allowed him to be with Miriam during the most fearful and disturbing days following the assault.

Miriam explained her experience in letters to a number of people from the Illinois congregation where they were members. One of the persons who responded was an elderly woman whose husband had recently died. Her own recent pain might have prompted her to respond to Miriam's letter. She had never experienced anything like rape, she wrote; therefore she could not understand what Miriam was going through. It must have been awful, she exclaimed, and wanted them to know she was praying for them and thinking of them often.

A woman at the Seminary, who didn't know the Nafzigers, sent cards to each of them. Each card was appropriate to the individual and expressed genuine caring for each. She said to Rodney, "I wish I could take away your hurt. How very much you are loved." And to Miriam she wrote, "Consider yourself hugged. If you ever need a friend and a listening ear (give a call)." The card to Rachel showed consideration and concern for her needs.

In spite of her calm demeanor throughout the rape, Miriam's life was shattered and rearranged. Insecurities and fears surfaced, which are common aftereffects for victims of rape. She had to find some way to make sense out of her disorganized and threatening situation. "During the three weeks after the assault, I was fortunate if there was an hour out of any one day when I didn't think about the rape. Throughout that stage I knew it wasn't my fault, but it was difficult to keep from blaming myself. I agonized over my actions that night. Maybe I could have done better, picked his pocket and found out who he was . . .

"I was unsure of myself because I felt such lack of control. Was life safe? If I dressed sloppily, could I protect myself from future attack? I had always connected rape with sex. However, I learned later that rape is more an act of violence and power than of sex."

Rodney, too, was traumatized by the event. When he looks over pages of thoughts he wrote throughout that year, he remembers the strong emotions that surfaced in him during those days.

"The first emotion I came in touch with the night of the rape was fear. This was new for me. It manifested itself in my religiously locking doors, day and night. I had never done that before.

"Anger was the most sustained emotion for me to process, express, and let go of. For years I had labeled anger as something negative, and I tended to take it inward. But that night, and many times afterward, I really raged off. I was angry with this man for coming into my house and hurting my wife. Then I was angry that he got away. I was mad at my helplessness. I, too, was a victim of disruption, both to my family and school life. I learned that the positive name of anger is energy, and that it is acceptable. Anger can be a resource when handled properly, and I have since used this awareness when counseling as a pastor.

"Such an event shakes up the whole family system. Books couldn't have taught me that. I was proud of the way Miriam handled the situation. In no way could I further victimize her by blaming her. During the rape, Miriam's talking to the rapist may have helped him to see her as a person and no longer as an object at his disposal. She gave him an alternative in a confronting and probing way, and she triumphed."

However, because the rapist was never identified or located, Rodney and Miriam had the ongoing frustration of not being able to communicate with the offender.

"I had to learn to bite my lip and give her space and time to process her own strong emotions. I had to learn to accept and try to understand her suspicion of men, which was extremely difficult. I also realized that she had to review her story over and over again for weeks and months. This meant backing off from my school life and studies. My professors were helpful in that, and I was grateful."

Miriam explains her own method of processing, pointing out that victims find their own methods for coping, or for denying, what has happened to them. 'I banged my fist on the counter one day and exclaimed, 'This is an awful thing that happened, but I'm going to make an education out of it!' " Rodney supported her in the study. She gathered books and media materials from a local rape aid center, libraries, and bookstores. What they learned was both shocking and comforting.

"As we read books and talked with our counselor, I felt like our blinders were being taken off," Rodney says. "I lost a trust that I had for society. It was disturbing to discover that our culture blames the persons who are raped and, thus, victimizes them further. Victims of rape and incest tend to hold the incident in secret because of this blaming attitude. It's overwhelming to me that these stories are buried and never processed, or processed poorly. For many, the pain accumulates as the secret is buried deeper, whereas our pain was lifted each time we shared. I can't imagine how Miriam would have been affected if she had kept this a secret. But the questions remain: with whom can I share who will really understand? How many people do I want to put through the trauma?"

Miriam's study brought up issues of the church's involvement in a rape victim's healing. Her concern is that the church provide an atmosphere where victims feel safe to share their stories. "I have learned that there is a lot of ignorance in the church about rape. It is crucial," she believes, "that persons in a congregation show interest in the mental and physical well-being of a rape victim." As Miriam observes in hindsight, she did not always have the ability to ask for what she needed. Because victims of violence need to recount their stories to others, she feels members of the faith community are well suited to meet this need. But she is concerned that they offer listening skills without solutions.

"It is important that the church handle victims with

gentleness through verbal or silent encouragement. It is better to acknowledge a person's hurt than to avoid them, merely because one doesn't know what to say or is afraid of saying the wrong thing.

"It is appropriate for a person to stay in contact with a victim through the stages of pain, asking questions like, 'What do you find the most difficult right now?' or 'What are you the most afraid of right now?' These are pertinent questions to be asked every two weeks. The answers will possibly change, which can be a sign of hope.

"I would never have thought it would literally take years to process a 15-minute encounter with a stranger—an encounter I supposedly WON! I handled it well, and I believe God helped me. But what does it feel like to a woman who doesn't win, or who is abused or raped repeatedly for years? How does the church respond to someone like that? Will the church be part of the solution, or contribute to the damage? I am thankful that no one responded to me by saying that the incident was God's will. For a rape victim to think that God had an agenda in rape is dangerous. If I had not been supported by family and the Seminary community, I may not have experienced God to be as kind and loving as I did."

Almost a year after the rape a Seminary professor invited Miriam to share her story and give a lecture about the subject. "Many people came and really wanted to know how they as ministers should care for a rape victim. I shared my encounter and gave information I had found through my extensive reading on the subject. Then Rodney spoke from the spouse's perspective and about pastoral response. For us, lecturing and sharing with people was very therapeutic."

"Throughout our recovery, the grace of God was mediated best through small clusterings of the faith community," says Rodney. "These clusters held special significance to me, because my trust in large structures, both society and church, was shaken. I also discovered the powerful supply of grace through our family of three."

Rodney bangs his fist on the table, "It's been an exciting journey, but I wouldn't wish anyone to discover it this way. This is NOT the way to discover this CRAP!" He bursts into laughter, but what he has said is sincere. The fear, distrust, and anxiety experienced by their family has drawn them tightly together, but none of them would have chosen to be brought together in this way.

An Open Door

They were both lying on the couch. Two little pink blankets I didn't notice until one of them moved. I was responding to a call for assistance. In the small bare trailer I found a distraught, weeping mother and five children, three still in diapers. There was not one bit of food in the house, and she had only six cloth diapers for all the babies. While I was there the landlord arrived to order her to vacate for nonpayment of rent. The twin girls were three weeks old. It was the fall of 1969.

My wife, Isabel, was hosting a Tupperware party that afternoon. Just as the guests started to arrive I brought her the two precious bundles, crying, hungry, and demanding a bath and dry diapers. Imagine the scene when one of the women came home with a baby and told her husband she won the door prize at the party!

Members of our church kept the babies for several weeks while helping the family get re-oriented. Several months later they moved on to a distant city and we lost touch.

In 1991 an advertisement appeared in our local paper with a picture of a lovely young lady. She had just turned 21 and had recently discovered she had a twin sister. They had both been placed for adoption and given to separate families. For a short time Jackson, Ohio, had been their home. Could anyone remember? We did.

To the People of Jackson, Ohio:

Last Friday I put an ad in the paper looking for my twin sister. Thanks to all the phone calls, I found my sister that night. We weren't supposed to be split up, but everyone knows how the system works. At age one, we were separated, and after 20 years apart we are together again. We were both brought up in good homes. We thank all those who made our reunion possible.

To Reverend Jim and Isabel Mullett and those ladies at the Tupperware party:
We would like to thank you personally for taking care of us for the couple of months that you had us. It's people like yourselves that make us see that there are caring people in the world.

Jim and Isabel Mullett
Jackson, Ohio

Baptism, For All the Right Reasons

Jim Reusser, Mennonite pastor, carried a secret for many years.

To anyone coming down the hall, I must have looked like an expectant father. True, I was pacing the floor of the maternity ward waiting room with the trademark expression of worry. Only one hour before I was relaxing into my seat at the music hall of the University of Waterloo, ready to enjoy a choral concert. Moments before the curtain rose, a colleague tapped my shoulder and told me I was needed at St. Mary's Hospital. Jane Bingeman, a member of the church where I served as pastor, had gone into labor, and her husband, Lawrence, was frantically trying to reach me. My friend relayed the message: the baby was not expected to live; would I baptize it?

Baptize? My mind leaped in mental gymnastics while I drove across town. I pondered the Mennonite practice of baptism in which individuals are baptized, not as infants, but as believers. This practice had become, in fact, a building block of the Mennonite faith. What would be the repercussions if I, a Mennonite pastor, performed an action so contradictory to a basic practice of the Mennonite church?

As a pastor, I had learned to expect anything, but I had never prepared myself for this kind of request. Jane was not of Mennonite background. She was raised in a tradition that performed infant baptism, and having her dying child baptized would provide her with comfort. My inner voice was telling me, "Go and support these people." At another level I was experiencing anxiety. "But does this mean I should baptize their baby?" I didn't want to cause a misunderstanding in the church.

It was a scary decision to make. But it became clear to me that I must perform this baptism for Jane's peace of mind. My concern about how the church would respond had to be secondary.

The next step was to rationalize my decision. I told myself that performing this rite would do nothing to the sick baby, but having the child baptized would be very important to the parents, especially to the mother. If the baby would live to adulthood, then there would be adequate time for me to talk about the choice to be baptized again.

Now, waiting alone in the maternity ward, I continued to ponder this pending baptism. What kind of ritual does a Mennonite pastor go through when baptizing a baby? I rehearsed in my mind what I might say and the gestures I might make.

My preparations were cut short when the double doors of the maternity ward flew open and a flurry of nurses and doctors swept into the waiting area. One of the nurses handed me a paper cup of water, for which I thanked her, and instinctively took a sip. When the warm water touched my lips, I knew that it was meant for baptizing, not for drinking.

With a flushed expression I turned to Jane, who was in the middle of the commotion on a stretcher. The reality of the moment had come to me the instant that warm water touched my tongue, and I was pulled into motion. The little girl was held up to me, and moments later I used the water I had been handed on her fragile forehead, saying, "I baptize you in the name of the Father, the Son, and the Holy Spirit." I could only imagine what that nurse was thinking, "What sort of ritual is this for the reverend to first drink and then baptize?"

I shared the story with my family. They believed I did the right thing but also found the drinking incident to be exceptionally funny. The story became a great source of humor among our family members. But for many years I was close-lipped about it outside our home, particularly because of my concern for the reputation of our congregation. I didn't want the wider church to misunderstand my action as a form of rebellion or disbelief in the practice of adult believer's baptism.

Ten years later I was traveling to a meeting in northern Canada with a ministerial committee from our local Mennonite conference. While we were driving, someone casually mentioned that I had not been interviewed by the conference since the time that our congregation decided to affiliate with both the Mennonite church and the General Conference Mennonite Church. The atmosphere was relaxed, and the men I was traveling with were friends I had known for years. They spontaneously, and quite informally, began to interview me in the car. The next thing I knew I was telling the story of my baptizing the Bingeman's baby.

As I talked I began to realize that over the years I had handled its confidentiality too seriously. The others in the car could tell I had been overly sensitive about it, and when I got to the part where I drank the baptismal water, their uproarious laughter set me at ease. At that point the mood shifted from informal to completely non-serious. We were zooming down the highway at 60 miles per hour when one of them said, "Thank you for the interview, Jim. Now could you step outside while we discuss your qualifications?" Once again, uproarious laughter resonated through the car.

Perhaps my own non-Mennonite background helped me understand Jane's point of view. In the 1920s my parents left the Mennonite Church because there were no opportunities in the church for my father to pursue vocal music as a full-time profession. Though my upbringing was mostly within the Presbyterian church where infant baptism was practiced, my parents maintained their Mennonite convictions. Neither I nor my siblings were baptized as infants. I only discovered as an adult that many of the teachings we learned in our family were rooted in Mennonite theology. Just as my parents continued to practice some of their Mennonite beliefs while attending a Presbyterian church, Jane maintained her belief in infant baptism while attending a Mennonite church.

As a Mennonite, I have always been committed to adult believer's baptism. But I have never had second thoughts about my choice to baptize the Bingemans' baby. It seemed like a Christ-like thing to do, which is the essence around which the Mennonite faith is anchored. I would do it again.

While hospitalized at Rockingham Memorial Hospital for chemotherapy, I frequently received Scripture verses related to healing and hope from a client of my husband's whom I had never met. It was as if the woman knew my daily emotional and physical situation because each set of verses was particularly appropriate for my emotional and physical status that day. To my surprise, I learned later that the woman could not read and was not familiar with the Bible. I was doubly inspired — both when I received the verses and when I discovered that God had chosen to use this illiterate woman to encourage me when I was deeply depressed.

Jan Glanzer
Harrisonburg, Virginia

An Invitation

Mary Ellen's* childhood is a blur of neglect and abuse. To the surrounding community her family appeared to be a typical Mennonite farm family. But her home was anything but a safe place. For almost 20 years, Mary Ellen's father abused her emotionally, physically, and sexually.

Mary Ellen believes that some of the leaders in their church knew that things were amiss in her home. When she was eight years old some members of the church and her parents' extended families tried to persuade her father to get treatment at Philhaven, a Mennonite mental health hospital, but he refused. Later, when the church would not allow him to participate in communion, he transferred the family's attendance to a Brethren in Christ church.

In the midst of these traumatic experiences, Mary Ellen's grandfather intervened by kidnapping her mother and brother from a school parent-teacher meeting. But that left Mary Ellen and her little brother alone with their father that night, and it was the first of many nights that he raped her.

"The house was never a safe place for me, and I felt lost and uncomfortable in school," says Mary Ellen. "I had difficulty concentrating and failed most of my major tests. I was labeled 'dumb' and held back. At home, my father's daily goal was to humiliate and degrade me and my siblings in any way he could. His abuses included locking me in the attic, urinating on me while I bathed, using sexual manipulation, and degrading me in front of the family at meals. I lived without privacy. I was also robbed of a relationship with my mother. My father forced me to report everything she did while he was away from home. I lived in constant terror of my father.

"After I was married, I attempted to help my youngest sister who was 14 and still living at home. I remembered how my life had been at age 14, and I asked the pastor of the Brethren in

Christ church where I grew up to find a family to be a role model for my sister. To my surprise, he declined without explaining why. I was deeply hurt and withdrew my membership. I felt the church had failed me by not saving me from years of abuse. Its teachings made me feel judged for abuse that was beyond my control, and now the church refused to be involved in the life of my sister. My suspicions seemed confirmed; the church did not care about me. I had a lot of anger toward God after that and didn't attend church for several years."

Mary Ellen found counseling and rehabilitation services through different avenues outside the church. A service called Rape Aid made arrangements for her to attend a six-week intensive therapy program in Arizona which started the first phases of her healing. "The program stressed that I needed a higher power in order to recover. I was encouraged to explore and build my own understanding of God, not necessarily based upon what I had been taught. This experience helped restore my interest in the church."

Two weeks after she returned from the program, her father committed suicide. His suicide further distanced her from her mother and siblings who blamed her for his death.

Mary Ellen sought counsel through the Brethren in Christ and Mennonite churches and began to share her story. Through these contacts she was asked to participate in the planning committee for a three-day conference about family abuse for the wider Brethren in Christ and Mennonite denominations. Being part of the committee held great significance for her. After a lifetime of being neglected and belittled, she felt heard and valued. Serving on the committee was a non-threatening invitation back into church related activities.

Mary Ellen told her story before an overflowing auditorium at the first group session of the conference.

"This was the first time I gave my story publicly, outside of therapy. The response was overwhelming. Throughout the weekend people continually came to me with their own stories. Now I knew I wasn't alone. The entire conference symbolized support for me, and the only negative feedback I got came from family members who were present."

Mary Ellen's involvement in the conference enabled her to begin freeing herself from some of the negative feelings she had about her childhood church. In turn, it allowed her to focus on positive parts of her Mennonite heritage.

Though she is estranged from most of her immediate family, she has established relationships with several relatives who have listened to and believed her story. She continues to nurture and strengthen her sense of womanhood, spirituality, and sexuality.

"I can relate to Christ. He was abused and betrayed like I was, and I can connect with his suffering. I refer to God as my Higher Power, and my self-image is ever growing. My Higher Power has placed people in my life and worked through them to help me heal. I don't think these people came into my life by chance. They fill me with strength and hope."

Mary Ellen added this postscript several days before her story was submitted for publication: "At this time, I don't feel so positive. I feel now that only a few Mennonites are with me for the long haul. I don't know how to change that."

* *Mary Ellen requested that her surname be withheld.*

As new immigrants, José and Seidy faced the usual obstacles one encounters in a new country and culture—language, resources, government and social systems, and employment. Naturally, they went through some low times, but, for the most part, they possessed positive, optimistic spirits. They sought out our Mennonite congregation, Holyrood Mennonite Church, and, to a large extent, this church became their family. José and Seidy gave what they could: a Spanish class for anyone interested, a painting by José for the church building, help with a primary Sunday school class, and service as church librarians. In turn, the church family gave them tuition and books for a two-year vocational training program, assistance in getting a car, and optical care for their children.

Ray Landis
Edmonton, Alberta

FROM MiliTARY
TO MENNONiTE

Rick and Pat Murphy first came to Martin's Creek Mennonite Church for an Easter sunrise service on a cold and snowy morning in 1975. The church members who shivered in the gray light of the cloud-hidden sunrise knew this young couple was different. Rick and Pat had bundled up their two toddler daughters, C.A. and Nissa, to bring them to church at the crack of dawn on the winter-like spring morning. That was unusual. Their personalities were as vibrant as their clothing, which looked like those advertised in stylish magazines, the kind of clothing that never graced the racks of local clothing stores.

Rick and Pat found the church's members a bit subdued, but they felt genuinely welcomed. They were attracted to the rural congregation where people seemed to relate to each other in a Christ-like manner. They had looked for this in other congregations, but had not found it. Elsewhere the emphasis seemed to be on seeking large memberships rather than a lifestyle modeled around Christ's teachings.

In addition to Rick's and Pat's different appearance, they brought with them divergent styles of worship, stemming from their experience in the Southern Baptist church and the free spirited charismatic movement of the early seventies. Furthermore, both had military upbringings which contrasted with the pacifist teachings of the Mennonites. It appeared that this couple and the rural Mennonite congregation would never be compatible. But the members of Martin's Creek Church embraced Rick's and Pat's differentness and used it creatively to enliven the congregation and its worship services.

Rick first came in contact with Mennonites when he met Nate and Vi Miller at the Baptist church he attended in Columbus, Ohio. It was they who first took him to the large Amish and

Mennonite community in Holmes County, Ohio, where Vi had grown up. Rick felt like he had stepped back in time, and he was immediately enamored.

The visit came just prior to Rick's joining the Navy in 1970. He was stationed in Norfolk, Virginia, but stayed in close contact with his Mennonite friends in Ohio. While his fellow naval colleagues modeled the trademark military haircuts and clean-shaven faces, Rick grew an Amish-style beard.

The independent charismatic movement was at its zenith, and its vibrant worship style also attracted Rick. Pat, a native of Norfolk, attended a charismatic church with her mother. Having been raised in the Southern Baptist church, Pat found the ways of the charismatic movement foreign. She and Rick discovered they had a lot of common questions about the church and God. They also found they had a common interest in each other and began to date. Pat and Rick believed in discipleship as evidence of one's relationship with Christ. And while they saw the membership of their church catapult, they observed little emphasis on discipleship.

When Rick's friends, Nate and Vi Miller, moved back to Holmes County, they encouraged him to come visit. After Rick and Pat were married, he took Pat to meet his friends in Ohio and experience the Mennonites and Amish. Likewise, Nate and Vi made trips to Norfolk to visit the Murphys.

In the spring of 1975, Pat's family went through a double trauma. Her older sister was killed in an automobile accident, and shortly afterward her father died suddenly from an aneurysm. Life in Norfolk became stifling and the Murphys wanted a change. The pressure of Pat's mother's grief and the weariness of city life contributed to their decision to move to Ohio. Nate and Vi suggested it first, and in a short time found them adequate housing. Within days the Murphys were en route to Ohio, car packed with all their belongings and their two toddler daughters.

Their decision to attend a Mennonite church was not an easy one. Rick wanted to find a church that would give them family-like support and provide substance that he hadn't found in the charismatic church in Norfolk. Pat still felt attached to the charismatic church, mainly for its dynamic style of worship.

To her, the ways of Martin's Creek felt foreign and the worship style too subdued. "The Mennonites seemed afraid to express any emotion or excitement about worshiping. Hymnal singing. No clapping. I thought, 'Ooo, this is dead.' I wondered what we were doing at this church with no feelings. I went in kicking, but accepted that Martin's Creek was where we needed to be."

What Martin's Creek lacked in energy, it compensated for in substance. The Murphys found friendship with other young parents, exchanging maternity clothing and sharing meals. In addition to their congregation, the Murphys made a wide variety of friends in the Amish and conservative Mennonite communities. They shared meals regularly and met for mutual guidance during decision making times.

As a teenager Rick felt being a Christian should be a daily commitment, not just a Sunday and Wednesday practice. When he asked a Sunday school teacher, "What does this Bible have to do with tomorrow?" the teacher was speechless. "That was a key moment for me," he says. "I kept looking for an answer to that question and knew I found it when we started to attend Martin's Creek. I don't think Martin's Creek took courses in assimilating new people. They just did what was natural to them; they took us in and loved us."

The church utilized Rick and Pat's gifts, asking them to teach Sunday School and serve as committee members. They tapped Pat's artistic talents for bulletin covers and banquet decorating. When the pastor invited Rick and Pat to become members of Martin's Creek, they were honest about their misgivings. Neither one was ready to accept the peace stance of the Mennonites, which opposed what they had been taught by their families. Rather than insist that they adhere to the peace theology before joining the church, the pastor heard their concerns and invited their membership. They agreed to continue studying the peace theology and joined the church in 1976.

Along that journey, church friends allowed Rick to be candid about his beliefs. One friend, in good humor, introduced Rick from the pulpit one Sunday saying, "That's Rick Murphy. He used to be in the Navy, but I love him anyway."

There were times, however, when Pat felt like an outsider.

Her southern upbringing taught her to dress nicely and look her best whenever she was in public. Her clothing and makeup appeared flashy to the Ohio community, and comments occasionally made her aware of this difference. "You're flamboyant," someone mentioned. Pat had not intended to draw attention to herself. In spite of these things, "we never felt we weren't acceptable as people," Pat says. "Nor did we feel pressure to change our style of dress. We felt we belonged."

After their third child was born, Pat decided to look for a job. She had been out of the work place for several years and needed counsel before entering the job market. She asked advice of a couple at Martin's Creek who owned a business. The couple, in turn, eagerly asked her whether she could do certain tasks. For each question, her answer was no. Not realizing that she was, in fact, being interviewed at that moment, Pat was surprised when they said,"We'll hire you anyway! " She was employed to write feature stories for a small newspaper, beginning the following week. Pat had no formal writing training, so the woman taught her interview techniques and critiqued her work.

"I never felt criticized," Pat says. "Her advice was constructive and positive. She encouraged a part of me that I didn't know I had."

In 1981 Rick was unemployed for a period of time, and their pastor invited him to attend a week-long pastors' seminar in Harrisonburg, Virginia. Having no excuse, Rick decided to go and felt the gentle nudge from his pastor to consider attending seminary. The timing didn't feel right to leave Holmes County, so Rick filed the thought in the back of his mind.

Later, when Martin's Creek fell into a period with no pastor, Rick was asked to give a sermon. His earlier notions about attending seminary rose to the surface again. A search committee began to look for pastoral candidates and came to Rick for advice. "Listen for the voice of the shepherd, God's calling to the congregation," he told them. "When you hear that you'll know it." Afterward a church leader patted Rick's back and said, "You'll make somebody a whale of a preacher some day."

"I was encouraged by his comment," Rick remembers, "but I was disappointed because I had secretly hoped that I might be called to serve as pastor of Martin's Creek."

But other circumstances arose. Eight days after Rick delivered his sermon Pat's stepfather died suddenly. Martin's Creek provided Rick and Pat with both the closeness and space they needed to grieve. Pat's mother needed them nearby, and their friends freed them to return to Norfolk. They would both work in her mother's business and live in a rental property her mother owned. On moving day their house was filled with friends who brought gifts, came to clean, prepare food, and load furniture onto the rental truck. It wasn't easy to leave.

"What we had seen at Martin's Creek," Pat says, "is what we wanted to do for my mother. Sadly, you can't transfer it to someone who doesn't know how to receive it. My stepfather's death brought old grief to the surface from my father's and sister's deaths. My mother was very hurt and angry and took it out on us."

The anger grew to the point where Rick and Pat could no longer work in the business or live in the rental house. High and dry in Norfolk, there was nowhere for them to go. Their first inclination was to move back to Ohio, but the sale of their house was already final, so those doors were closed. They did return to Holmes County for advice. Nate and Vi pointed out one open door. With no jobs, housing, or ties, they told Rick he had no excuse *not* to go to seminary.

Rick chose Eastern Mennonite Seminary in Harrisonburg, Virginia, the site of the pastor's conference he had attended several years before. In contrast to their move from Ohio, Rick and Pat loaded a moving van alone, preparing to leave coastal Norfolk for the mountains of western Virginia.

Housing and enrollment came fairly easily, but finances remained in question. Rick refused a financial aid package that would leave them in debt for years after his graduation. He decided the funds would have to come in some other way. On July 4 the family sat on the porch of their rental house, wondering whether they had made the right decision. In order for Rick to go to school full-time, Pat would have to work full-time. Pat felt she was betraying their children because she wouldn't be home when they came home from school.

After classes began at the seminary, some friends from Martin's Creek came to visit, their car brimming with packages from church members. Besides the abundance of food and gifts they brought with them, they informed Rick and Pat that Martin's Creek wanted to help them financially. They wanted to know how Pat's earnings compared to Rick's tuition and their family expenses. The church would try to pay the difference.

After that, checks arrived monthly, their sums varying between $300 and $600. The church had designated $100 a month in the budget, and anything above that came from individuals. The Murphys always had enough money to cover their seminary and household bills. The generosity continued when they traveled to Holmes County for Christmas. The family that hosted them also included them in their family gift exchange and holiday meal.

While in Harrisonburg, Rick served as an intern to the pastor of a Mennonite church. It was good practical experience in addition to his long hours of lectures and study. When the second Christmas of their two seminary years approached, Rick realized they had no extra money for gifts. He dreaded telling their children, but finally admitted that if they got anything for Christmas it was provided by God. Some members of Harrisonburg Mennonite found out what the children wanted and gave each member of the family presents. Prior to Christmas, certified checks arrived from Ohio. Rick and Pat were overwhelmed to be loved and treated like family during a time when they were estranged from their own families. "Our Mennonite friends didn't want us to live on the minimum," says Rick. "It was clear to us that they wanted us to enjoy our seminary experience."

The Holmes County network actively guided and supported the Murphys when Rick interviewed for a pastoral position in Lancaster County, Pennsylvania, in 1985. Rick was excited, but Pat remained cautious. During the interviews Pat dressed as she normally did. "I didn't want there to be any questions about where I stood. I wore jewelry and makeup. In one discussion the issue of a head covering came up and we said that if I was expected to wear a covering we had made a mistake in coming there."

Rick was offered, and accepted, the position of half-time pastor of Mountville Mennonite Church and half-time resource person to the local Lancaster Mennonite Conference. Mountville church was established in 1898 and almost closed in 1980. At that point the bishop invited nine families who had formerly attended to come back. Six of them did. The Church was still getting back on its feet when Rick and Pat came.

Two weeks before Rick's ordination, a bishop asked Pat why she wasn't wearing a covering. He also asked her to wear less makeup and to remove her earrings.

"Rick told the bishop that I wasn't going to change who I was, and, if he wanted me to conform, then he shouldn't ordain Rick. Later another person saw me wearing shorts and told Rick that wouldn't go over well in the conference. I got the message that the only way I would be acceptable was if I changed."

The Murphys didn't ignore those exchanges, but believed that the people at Mountville would learn to accept them as the Mennonites in Ohio had. Yet tensions continued. Rick was hired to bring life back to a struggling congregation, but when he initiated changes that brought growth, conflicts and misunderstandings developed as well.

Pat soon observed that her every action and word, both in and out of the church, were judged according to her role as a Mennonite pastor's wife, not as Pat Murphy. She felt considerable inner turmoil about what it meant to be a Mennonite pastor's wife. At work she kept that part of her identity hidden so that she could be herself among her co-workers. For the first year of Rick's pastorate, Pat spent hours renovating their older home, keeping to herself, and only fulfilling church duties that were absolutely necessary.

Despite that, the early years of Rick's pastorate were rich. Many members of the church were excited about his approach to ministry. Rick's candid sermons challenged people to explore their faith and exercise it in their daily lives. He enjoyed engaging people in conversation. "I learned through my previous work to listen to people. If you let people talk about who they are, you will learn a lot about them and will eventually earn the right to speak into their lives. We became listeners in the congregation and in the community. One night a neighbor came over to our porch and we talked for several hours. I just asked him questions about himself. He finally asked me, 'What do you do?' I told him I was a pastor. He nearly fell over. The word got out that I was an accepting person and a listener. That's how many people came into the church."

Simultaneously, some of the long time members were uncomfortable with the numerous changes that happened at Mountville. The congregation was divided by different needs and agendas, and Rick seemed to walk on a tightrope between.

"I think anyone who would have come there would have had problems, but I was part of the problem. There were many roots to the conflicts. My leadership style was different from that of my predecessors. Whereas Mennonites tend to handle conflict passively, I am assertive. I got in and assessed the situation. I heard many concerns in the congregation that needed to be addressed so I came to the leadership team and said, 'Here's what I'm hearing. What are we going to do about it?' That took them aback. I was perceived as being authoritarian because I was strong. I didn't say, 'I think we might, should, maybe could possibly do this.' I said, 'I think we ought to do this.' You had to know me to know that I would back off just as quickly as I came on. But my assertiveness was interpreted as inflexibility.

"Another issue was church growth. In the five years I was pastor the congregation grew from 80 to 130. This meant that decision-making processes and power structures needed to change to accommodate the growth. New people dilute things, and this was a threat to some long-time members since many of the newcomers were from non-Mennonite background. The former pastor was part of the leadership team, and others in the congregation still had a commitment to him.

"As pastor I encountered many situations where I had no idea what to do. At one point I had five church members in different stages of divorce. In my job history I always had a supervisor to go to. But now I had no mentor, no one to go to for advice. So I called every community and church resource I knew. I was on the cutting edge while at the same time I was fighting with a group in the congregation who didn't like the way things were."

In the spring of 1990 some Mennonite pastors asked Rick to join them in a church planting endeavor. Rick drove across town processing the events at Mountville and the possible prospect."I was discouraged because I wanted to serve at Mountville, yet it felt like so many people didn't want me there. That was on a Monday. On Wednesday my bishop came to me and told me that someone from the congregation gave him two tapes of my sermons from that month and said they weren't biblical. He said he listened to the sermons and talked with two people from the congregation. I was shocked that he didn't send the people to discuss the sermons with me, and that he didn't talk with me before consulting others in the church. Throughout my pastorate I welcomed criticism and discussion of my sermons, and many people shared their thoughts with me. I was both sad and angry that someone who didn't agree with me went to the bishop without first talking with me."

Rick's emotional health was suffering. Little of his energy, other than his expressed frustration, followed him home to Pat and their children. That weekend Pat came to her wits' end. "Rick gave all his time to the church. Instead of working half-time as pastor and half-time as resource person, he worked time and a half for both. In a roundabout way, we got the message that you had to sacrifice family to be a minister. But I finally told Rick that he married me and had children before he was a pastor. He had made those commitments first, and we were being neglected. I told him I would leave him if things didn't change."

Pat's intervention was necessary for Rick to look clearly at the conflicts that were building within the congregation and within his family. The following Sunday he addressed some of the congregational conflicts from the pulpit. Rick then asked whether they were ready to work with him and the elders in reconciliation. He also asked if they would support the elders in disciplining persons who Rick felt were causing dissention in the congregation. Seventy-five percent of the people said, "Yes, we want to work toward reconciliation." However, it was less clear how the congregation felt about the call for disciplinary action.

The leadership team met with Rick on Tuesday evening and committed themselves to reconciling the conflicts in the church.

But they also expressed their disapproval of Rick's calling for discipline.

The elders recommended that an outside consultant team mediate, and the congregation agreed. Rick was granted a three-month leave of absence on full salary so that he could deal with personal and family issues and work closely with the consultant team.

When the consulting team completed its work in July of 1990, Rick resigned. He felt that by continuing in the pastorate he would risk further damage to his family. "I've seen pastors stay in limbo for years, and there is evidence of it in their fragmented families," Rick says. "I didn't want that to happen to us, but I'm not sure I got out soon enough. For the last year and a half I've tried to rebuild my relationship with our kids. They have a lot of anger, not only toward the church, but toward me and how I handled them while I was a pastor."

After Rick resigned, the congregation decided to extend his salary for another two months since he was leaving because of congregational problems. Rick and Pat continued to live in the town of Mountville but felt isolated from the congregation and larger church conference they had served for five years.

In January 1992, the dean of Eastern Mennonite Seminary invited Rick to come to the ministers' week. The theme was Hurting Pastors. "I told him it was too little and too late. I said, 'I'm working full-time. I can't afford to take off work to go to ministers' week. I'm not a minister anymore.' I told him that I went to seminary to prepare for pastoral ministry. I came with some emotional problems. I got a degree and left with some emotional problems. Then in the pastorate, due to the pressures of ministry, my emotional problems were intensified. My experience at Mountville helped me to see I needed help, which is good, but I wish I hadn't had to look outside the Mennonite church for counseling. Now I'm a former pastor with a Master's degree, seminary training and experience, and I'm selling cars. I really needed a seminar on hurting pastors two or three years ago. The dean thanked me for being honest. He really understood and was sensitive."

In the spring of 1992, East Chestnut Street Mennonite

Church in Lancaster, Pennsylvania, invited Rick and Pat to lead a Sunday school class on the topic of building trusting relationships in the church. The lively discussions and relationships that grew out of the class reaffirmed to the Murphys that they had something valuable to contribute, although they continued to be uncertain about their future involvement in the church.

While teaching the class, they attended the first Easter service since Rick resigned at Mountville. "It was supposed to be the biggest day of celebration, Easter. I was thinking, 'This has almost nothing to do with my life now compared to how it did before. How does that fit?' We've decided to move back to Ohio to be among close friends and have the support we need to heal. Where we'll be in five years, I don't know. Will I ever be in ministry again? I don't know."

Nine years after leaving Ohio, Rick and Pat Murphy prepared to move back to Holmes County. On moving day neighbors and several members of the recent Sunday school class came to help. A few people from the Mountville congregation called the Murphys to ask whether they could come and help. Pat declined the offers, saying it would be too painful. However, on moving day one couple brought them some food and several others showed up unexpectedly to load the truck.

Rick's pastorate at Mountville has resulted in painful fallout for him and his family. The experience rattled Rick and Pat's faith in the Mennonite church where they had once found sanctuary and acceptance. Mountville Mennonite Church also suffered, but Ray Reitz, the current pastor, says the church would not be where it is today without Rick's past leadership. Rick identified the congregation's destructive practice of sweeping conflict under the rug rather than facing it. Today the congregation is much more able to face conflict head-on. There is still much diversity among the members, but the bickering and fighting have stopped.

Three years later the Murphys are still trying to reconcile their broken relationship with the Mennonite church.

Bethany Birches Camp is grateful for nearly ten years of giving that we received from Omar Zook. We met Omar when Jim was a Voluntary Service (VS) administrator in Reading, Pennsylvania. Omar worked at a prison halfway house where Jim placed VSers from time to time. When Jim first met Omar his wife was very ill with Multiple Sclerosis, and Omar needed to push her everywhere in a wheelchair. He began to build a house for the two of them which would be entirely equipped for her needs with railings in every room and an elevator. He spent all his extra hours working on this house.

We moved to Vermont to pastor Bethany Mennonite Church and direct Bethany Birches Camp. We learned the sad news that Omar's wife died right after he completed the house. On a whim we decided to invite Omar to come to camp for the summer. He was about 75 the first year he came and in great physical shape. He was in charge of camp maintenance.

Omar took an immediate interest in the camp, and wanted to give his time and finances to improve our facilities. The camp kitchen was in very poor condition, and Omar brought it up to code, replacing things and making repairs. Every year he took on a project and gave toward it until it met the standards. He built a maintenance shed and gave thousands of dollars toward the renovations of our camp cabin. In addition, he donated the use of his van each summer. We used it to transport kids and haul canoes or supplies.

In return, the camp offered Omar a place to be in a community. Each summer he talked about his wife and continued to deal with his grief. This is a place where he came to work through that sad part of himself. He found comfort here.

Each evening Omar sat on the porch of the cabin and watched the kids' activities down below in the field. When there were troublemakers, we often sent them up to Omar who talked with them and listened. We don't know what he said, but they always calmed down.

At a time when Omar needed to be cared for, he chose to give. Bethany Birches Camp and many lives have benefited from his choice.

Jim & Aldine Musser
Bridgewater Corners, Vermont

Sharing
a Decision

"Your action feels like taxation without representation!" declared one person in response to Sharing Programs' announcement of a 300 percent increase in their Liability Plan's assessments for Mennonites living in Philadelphia. "Why didn't you talk with us before you raised the assessment? I thought you were a 'sharing' program! This feels like we are being punished." Philadelphia area pastors and Brotherly Aid Liability Plan members spoke with considerable concern at a meeting in Philadelphia in September 1991.

The Brotherly Aid Liability Plan, a division of Sharing Programs of the Lancaster Mennonite Conference, Inc., faced a dilemma: what is the best way to help a large group of people share one another's burdens when some in the group are consistently needing proportionally more help than others?

The Liability Plan provides an alternative to motor vehicle liability insurance for persons in the Mennonite family of churches in Pennsylvania. From its beginning in 1955 until 1991, everyone paid the same basic assessment for enrolling a passenger vehicle. And, for most of its history, the Plan's rates tended to be considerably lower than rates charged by insurance companies. However, in recent years, the Plan needed to raise its rates significantly, at the same time insurance companies were required by law to lower their rates. As a result, some members began to leave the Plan.

After analyzing the Plan's claims data, the Administrative Committee decided that rates in all areas must go up so that each area bears more of its share of the costs. Yet even with that corrective, members in Philadelphia would pay proportionately less of their full costs than members from more rural areas pay of theirs. But the committee assumed that participants would leave the Plan if the cost was more than comparable insurance costs. The decision was made in July, 1991, for implementation with the October 1 assessments. Philadelphia rates were to change from $100 to $284 for a six-month enrollment period.

Liability Plan staff, anticipating that the nearly 300 percent increase might be a problem for members in Philadelphia, arranged a meeting with pastors and other interested persons to talk about the situation. The staff was not prepared for the level of emotions at the meeting. Several members who came were angry. "The dramatic increase with little advance notice and no prior consultation feels like punishment, not mutual aid! " said one frustrated member. Another member said the increase felt like a slap in the face, and one more tug for persons to move out of the city. "Rural Mennonites do not seem to want to support those of us in the city." And, "It's like city government: higher taxes and fewer services." A teacher in a Christian school said, "Our budget is so tight that we must do very careful planning from year to year in order to make ends meet." He said that his family's budget simply could not absorb such a jump in assessments. Someone suggested that Philadelphia should have a member on the Sharing Programs Board. Participants in Philadelphia should have direct access to the decision making process of Sharing Programs, and Sharing Programs should be more in touch with the plight of Mennonites in the city.

The staff soon set aside their agenda for the meeting in order to listen to what members were saying. Participants expressed appreciation for having been heard. Yet someone quickly added, "But what are you going to do about it?" The staff assured them that their concerns would be taken to the Administrative Committee and Board. But they made no promises to reverse the decision on assessment rates.

During the car ride back to Lancaster, the staff tried to understand what they had heard. Pain had been clearly expressed by Plan members—the pain of bearing such a large and unexpected financial burden without time to prepare. "We were caught up short. The members were right about the lack of sensitivity and concern the Plan had shown them by making such a demand," commented one staff person. "Is there any way we can change the decision? How are we going to respond?"

The next day in the office, those who were part of the Philadelphia meeting reported to the General Administrator and other staff members. During the next few days they all spent considerable time trying to find a way to bring relief to the Philadelphia participants. While the staff felt the anxiety and anger of the brothers and sisters in Philadelphia, they were also keenly aware of the reality of the rate problem for the majority of Plan participants.

After much thought and prayer, the staff and Administrative committee agreed to roll back the Philadelphia area assessments by 50 percent for a one-year period, during which time they would conduct a thorough review. The main purposes of the review were to see if participants would leave the Plan if costs were higher then comparable insurance and to try to discover an alternative way of handling the assessments. The review process involved two aspects: sending a questionnaire to all participants and conducting a series of 16 meetings throughout the region to allow direct feedback and input.

The questionnaire responses indicated a strong (67 percent) preference for varying the rates based on claims' experience. At the same time, members expressed an equally strong desire to help other members who could not pay part or all of their assessment. Most of the 500 members attending the area meetings supported the questionnaire responses. At the end of the yearlong review, the Administrative Committee decided to keep the assessment system based on claims' experience. The Plan needed to keep its good drivers.

At the same time, the Committee encouraged revitalization of the Special Assistance fund to enable Sharing Programs to respond to persons who had low incomes or were experiencing financial difficulties.

Also, in the spring of 1992, a participant from Philadelphia was appointed to the Sharing Programs Board, due, in part, to a recognition of the need for urban representation on the Board.

At this point, the dilemma of how to help share burdens when some members of the group consistently have a greater need seems to be solved. Assessments are higher for the group with higher expenses, but financial assistance is available for any participants who are unable to meet their costs.

All summer we had been trying to sell our house on Orange Street. Our goal was to sell before the cold weather set in. We had found a house on City Mill Road that we thought would be suitable for our family, and we made a substantial down payment for its purchase, thinking that we could sell our house that summer. But our house did not sell. By September our agreement with the realtor had expired and the For Sale sign was taken down. Discouragement set in.

Our family huddled on a number of occasions for meditation and prayer and for sharing our feelings. However, our middle child, Talita, constantly reminded us, "Don't worry, God will sell our house." She said this even in the hottest months of July and August when it seemed totally impossible.

In the meantime, we received a call from the owners of the City Mill Road house, saying that they would lower the price by $20,000. We felt that we still could not swing it financially, but we made a counteroffer, saying that we would buy it if they would take an additional $20,000 off the reduced price. They said they could not do that, so we asked for our money back.

Ten families looked at the City Mill Road house in a two week period, but no one placed a bid. The owners called us back, saying they would accept our offer ($40,000 under the original price). We were then able to pass some of our financial blessings to Rose Martin, a single woman who has lived sacrificially and shared generously with others. We sold her our Orange Street house for $15,000 below market value.

Yes, God honored Talita's faith. God did sell our house, but he did it through his people. It was, indeed, a miracle.

Lawrence Chiles
Lancaster, Pennsylvania

A Door to a Community: A Store and a Church

Gladys Miller Mast recalls the welcome her family received as newcomers to a rural community.

In 1954, my first husband, Willis Miller, and I moved to Petoskey, Michigan, at the invitation of Ivan Weaver, pastor of the Petoskey Mennonite Church. Shortly after we arrived Ivan asked us to look for areas where another Bible school could be held in the summer. Meanwhile, Willis and I became active in the Petoskey Church, teaching and leading the youth.

In 1955 Willis became ill with a chronic inner ear infection. While he was hospitalized, his roommate told him about a hill near the town of Stutsmanville with a view of five islands in Lake Michigan. When Willis was released he told me that he wanted to take the family to the hill for a picnic. I was less than enthusiastic, because I worked nights at a nursing home and cared for our three children during the day, but I consented. We loaded our family into the car and headed toward Lake Michigan. We did not see those five islands, but we did have a nice picnic. What I remember most clearly is the drive we took through the town of Stutsmanville. We noticed a church building surrounded by tall weeds, the evidence of long-standing vacancy. Willis remembered Ivan's request to look for potential locations for further outreach, so we inquired with a neighbor about using the church building. He directed us to a member of the church board.

Several weeks later we returned to survey the community. Approximately 20 families, with a large population of children, lived within two miles of the church. Within a year of our picnic day, we opened the doors of the church for summer Bible school. We traveled 20 miles from Petoskey to coordinate activities in

Stutsmanville, and other Mennonites came from Petoskey and Brutus, Michigan, and from Goshen, Indiana, to help with the classes. We learned to know members of the community through their children. Three Christian woman volunteered to help with the Bible school and Sunday school the following year.

After the first summer of Bible school, some local families asked if we could start having Sunday morning services in the church. Ivan could not manage preaching two sermons every Sunday and encouraged Willis to take leadership in Stutsmanville. The Indiana-Michigan Mission Board began the process of buying the church.

On the first Sunday morning, 30 people attended the service at Stutsmanville Mennonite Church. Willis preached and I told the children a story. We traveled back and forth Sunday after Sunday, and soon the attendance increased to an average of 40. In the beginning, several Mennonites from Petoskey and Goshen, Indiana, came to help us get the church program established. Soon, more of the local men and women were teaching Sunday school classes and helping with the summer Bible school.

That first winter we asked a neighbor to stoke the fire in the church stove so the church would be heated by the time we arrived from Petoskey. Though he didn't attend the services, this neighbor faithfully started the fire each Sunday and told us he supported the church in the community.

Soon before the church was purchased in 1958, Willis became ill again. This time he had a nagging tonsil infection that would not heal. A doctor finally diagnosed the illness as Hodgkin's Disease and told Willis he could expect to live for only two more years. The diagnosis made Willis all the more committed to the new church and to the people within its proximity. He spent many hours visiting local families to get to know them personally and to invite them to attend.

In mid-1958, the house across the road from the church was put up for sale. One side of the house was a country store with a Phillips 66 gas pump in front. We felt it was time to move into Stutsmanville and become more active in the daily life of the community, so we purchased the house and store.

Our store turned out to be a door to the entire community.

People gathered there just to talk and visit. In addition to our work at the church, the store provided a more informal atmosphere for interacting with local people.

After we moved, we decided it was time to make some repairs on the church building. A work group came up from Indiana to put shingles on the church roof. The next year, a group came to scrape the peeling paint and to repaint the siding. Men and women from Stutsmanville came to work and prepare meals during the remodeling.

I have fond memories of church life in the new congregation. We established many friendships and developed traditions which brought us together, one being the ringing of the church bell each Sunday morning. Often the community children came and took turns pulling the rope to ring the bell 30 rings, sometimes pulling so hard the bell got stuck upside down until someone climbed into the steeple to right it. We soon started communion services and also went to the homes of several elderly community members so they could receive communion. A women's group met regularly in each other's homes to sew for people in need. At Thanksgiving we held a feast and program for the entire community.

We invested a lot of our time in the youth of Stutsmanville. Sometimes as many as 25 teenagers came to church on a Sunday morning, and they met for monthly activities. Often they did things with the youth from the two other Mennonite congregations nearby.

Willis' illness appeared to be under control during our transition into life in Stutsmanville. He spent many hours visiting the elderly people in the community, yet was a real friend to people of all age groups. But again, the disease showed its effects, and, after the birth of our son, Willis was hospitalized. It turned out that he spent more than half of our son's first year in the hospital in Ann Arbor.

The community came to my aid with child care and running the store while I visited Willis. One family took care of the baby at a moment's notice, and another family took the girls into their home when I needed to be away. Another neighbor, a native American, took care of business at the store and brought me firewood in exchange for groceries.

Each time Willis went to Ann Arbor for treatment, it cost us 100 dollars. On one occasion he needed to go, but we could only scrape 80 dollars together. In spite of the shortage, we loaded the car and planned for Willis to go early the next morning. During the night someone slipped an envelope under our door. The envelope contained 20 dollars.

Once when Willis was able to come home from the hospital, a teenage girl from the community made a banner for him. The sign saying, "Welcome Home Preacher!" greeted him over the stairway of the church. He was exhausted and sick from treatment, but the banner helped to lift his spirits.

Near the end of his life, Willis needed all his strength just to preach a sermon. He would come home from church completely exhausted. Even though he was extremely weak, he continued to drive the local school bus. He would eat breakfast, vomit, and then go on the bus route. He wanted to continue driving because it gave him contact with the school children and the community.

Willis died in December of 1960 at age 34. He lived four years after the diagnosis of Hodgkin's Disease, two years longer than expected. He dedicated those years to the congregation and community at Stutsmanville.

Living at the store turned out to be a real blessing. As a young widow with small children, I was able to be at home with my family, yet still receive income. One woman in our church helped me cope with being alone. She was also a widow with three children. When I needed a friend to cry and pray with, she would come. Other friends took care of the baby on Sunday mornings so I could teach Sunday school. The people in Stutsmanville clearly cared about me, and it was evident by their many acts of kindness throughout Willis' illness and after his death.

The current pastor, Ed Warner, was ordained in 1971 to serve as pastor of the Stutsmanville congregation. He was one of the boys who attended the first Bible school. Today the congregation is vibrant and growing, with over 200 people attending on a Sunday morning. The health of the congregation is the legacy of many generous people who, over the years, gave their time and energy to bring a bit of God's kingdom to the Stutsmanville community.

As I approached the outskirts of town on my way to work one day, I pressed the brakes to stop at a red light, but my car kept moving. I veered to the left to avoid hitting the car in front of me, and by grabbing the emergency brake was able to stop the car.

A truck was approaching the intersection at the same time, and the driver cursed at me for running the red light. "Oh God," I prayed, "please hold this old car together until I've finished nurses' training and can help Mom and Dad buy a better car."

My parents had worked hard all their lives, but misfortunes had befallen them and they never had a surplus of money. My father was a deacon for over 30 years without pay and often left his work to help someone in need. I had only 10 months left in training and was looking forward to helping them financially.

Two months later I was charting in the nurses' station when I noticed my father standing in the doorway. He seemed upset, unusual for his typically calm demeanor. I asked him what the trouble was.

"You couldn't guess what happened today." I braced myself for a crisis. Instead, he told of a phone call he received, asking him to go to the local Oldsmobile dealer that afternoon. When he got there, he was met by the car salesman and a gentleman from our church. They showed him a brand new car and said that if he signed a few papers, it would be his. The man from our church told him, "I'm on the road making money and you're on the road, also, but working for the church. I want to give this car to you in appreciation for what you do for the congregation."

I recalled my earlier prayer asking God to hold our old car together until I could help purchase another. Instead, God gave abundantly above all that I could ask or think.

Ruth Kennel
Harrisonburg, Virginia

Adopting Convictions

"I have always wanted to adopt children," says Sue Rush. "Probably my father influenced me the most in that wish. He always wanted to help children, and there were always extra kids at my parents' house."

Sue's husband, Don, came to that conviction more slowly. They talked about it as they dated, got married, and had children. When their second child, Nathan, was born with health problems, it confirmed their decision not to have any more biological children, but to adopt.

That choice has greatly enriched Sue's life. Her interracial family has undergone tough times because of racial prejudice, Nathan's health needs, and the emotional trauma of Sue's and Don's separation and divorce. The Mennonite church has offered Sue and her family both comfort and pain in relation to racism, divorce, and physical disabilities. It has been a journey not only for Sue and her children, but for the members of their current congregation, First Deaf Mennonite Church.

Sue's strong convictions for nonviolence and peace led her and Don from a Baptist church to the Alpha (NJ) Mennonite Church where Henry Swartley was pastor. Henry and his wife, Ida, became mentors for the young couple and were particularly supportive of their desire to adopt children.

When another pastor contacted Henry, searching for potential parents to adopt the baby of a young pregnant woman, Henry was in touch with Sue and Don. He counseled them as they tried to decide about adopting the woman's baby when it was born.

"Eliza's mother was white and her father Tanzanian," says Sue. "Race was not an issue for me in adopting Eliza. We were thrilled to have her join our family." Henry and Ida drove with them to Philadelphia to pick up four-day-old Eliza. She joined eight-year-old Pam and six-year-old Nathan as a much loved member of the family.

"Alpha Mennonite supported us in every way. Eliza was never excluded because of her race and had a lot of good friends there." The church was equally affirmative when they adopted Martin four years later. He is black, white, Korean, and Hispanic, and is now an energetic 11-year-old. Sue and Don named him Martin Henry after her father and Henry Swartley.

Two other children became part of the family, though they were never officially adopted. "Jimmy came to us through the Department of Mental Retardation. We were supposed to have a client-type relationship with this boy, but it grew to be more than that. I love Jimmy. He was in our home for five years and is still in contact with us.

"Maria joined us after we moved to Paradise, Pennsylvania, the week before she started as a freshman at Lancaster Mennonite High School. Someone from the school office called us and said, 'We have a girl here whom we would like to put in a home rather than in the dorm. She is Puerto Rican and we knew you have an interracial family. Would you take her?' We did. She and I have a mother-daughter relationship."

Sue and Don began to attend First Deaf Mennonite Church, a congregation that holds services for both deaf and hearing. "One of the reasons we were drawn to First Deaf was for Nathan's benefit. We figured a congregation that strives to meet the needs of deaf people would be accepting of Nathan's differences. Nathan is learning disabled. He has some fine motor skill deficiencies and has been in special education since preschool. He is 21 now and doing vocational training in grounds maintenance.

"As we hoped, the members of First Deaf have been truly accepting of Nathan. One family in particular, Phyllis and Jim Oswald and their children, have reached out to Nathan. Their daughters are his age and invite him to go places with them, such as school plays and visiting their cousins. Nathan likes to hang out with the kids, but he doesn't have a lot of friends because of his disabilities, and the Oswalds have always included him.

"Cindy Wert is another person who includes Nathan in her activities. She's been in college for a year, and now she's in voluntary service in New York, but whenever she's here she takes a day and spends it with Nathan. The last time she was home she called him and said, 'Okay Nathan, when are we going out?' They went out to dinner and saw a movie. She's not embarrassed to be with him.

"Nathan is a joy. He is sensitive to people's needs, especially mine. He can tell when I need a hug. He has extra love to give to others."

Though Nathan's experience in school and church has been fairly smooth, Eliza and Martin have faced racial prejudices in both settings. Sue observes both subtle and overt racism.

"When the kids were little, everybody loved them. When they got to be preteens, the children's friends and their parents hesitated about whether they wanted them overnight at their houses. Then when they got to where Eliza is now—high school—there was more tension in their relationships with both kids and teachers.

"Eliza has to take more prejudice than Martin probably ever will, because Eliza looks black. She is 15 years old and has to deal with all kinds of subtle prejudice. There are many examples of racism that you can miss if you're not in tune to them. Most of the subtleties are exclusion, the feeling of not being totally accepted because you're different. They include not being invited to parties or, as a family, not being invited to someone's house.

"Things happen to Eliza in the hallways at school. Someone will pass her and say, just so she can hear it, 'Watch out, Eliza; I'll get you.' Some are brazen enough to say things outright—commenting about 'niggers' so Eliza will hear it. If she wants to date someone, people give that person a hard time, telling him why he can't like her. A lot of times these are kids from Christian families.

"You come to expect kids to be insensitive, but some of Eliza's teachers have given her trouble, including one who is a Christian. It is hard when you know that person is a leader in the church but can't accept a child because of the color of her skin. A teacher in intermediate school made a point of embarrassing Eliza in front of the other students. She questioned him a couple of times about whether his practice was a racial issue. He didn't say yes or no, but he never denied it.

"Society does dictate racist attitudes. When we moved here, I tried to find a hairdresser for Eliza, because not everybody can cut her hair. The first woman we went to, who was black, gave me a very hard time for having Eliza. She thought Eliza should be with a black family and said I shouldn't have her. I couldn't wait to get out of there, and we've never gone back. You get it on both sides, from whites and blacks. For the last three or four years, Eliza has had a hard time with one boy at school. He just found out during basketball season that Eliza was adopted. For some reason that made it all okay and he seems more able to accept her."

Other racial harassment occurred while Eliza was playing softball. Throughout a game, three mothers and a teenage girl from the opposing team repeatedly yelled racist comments to her. "They called her names like 'jungle bunny.' I even heard the girl call her 'nigger.' When Eliza hit the ball and was running to first base they really heckled her. It was hard for me to stay in my seat. Our coach's wife got up and quietly went over and sat in front of them. That stopped them for that game."

Later in the season when they played the same team for a second time, Eliza's teammates stuck up for and protected her. Without saying anything prior to the game, family members of her teammates sat around the women who had caused problems at the earlier game, and the referees agreed to remove them from the stands if they heckled Eliza again.

"I don't step into my kids' conflicts easily, but there are many times when I have wondered if I should, especially when they are racial. Eliza always says, 'No, I will handle it.' She really amazes me. She has developed strong convictions and has grown as a person. The older she gets the more she sticks up for herself. I don't want her to feel like she always has to—she can reach out for help. At the same time, it is something she will probably have to deal with for the rest of her life. We talk about it a lot, which I think is a plus.

"It's even harder for Eliza to tolerate racism in the church than it is for me. But that is my biggest tension point. It is one thing I can never accept. Eliza senses some racism at First Deaf. There's a boy in her Sunday school class who is outwardly prejudiced toward her. They've discussed it in the class, and the teacher has talked with me about it.

"Also, when my oldest daughter Pam was in high school, she went to a joint youth group meeting at another church where they were discussing dating, including interracial dating. One girl, whose father was a Mennonite pastor, said her parents would not let her date a boy that was Hispanic, because of his race. The youth leader said that she, too, did not believe in interracial dating. She said she knew a black woman who married a white man, and that they had brown children with red hair. That was her reason. Pam came home furious. I told her she must have misunderstood. I called the woman to find out what she meant, and she told me the same story. It upset me that she was leading the youth group at a local Mennonite church and feeding teenagers those sorts of views."

In 1989 Don unexpectedly and abruptly left the family. When Sue recovered from the initial shock, she had to face an aftermath of massive debts, emotional stress, and question marks about their 20-year marriage. The children felt abandoned, confused, and hurt. The separation eventually ended in divorce. "I'm not sure that I really know, or that I'll ever know, what led to the divorce, so I'm guessing.

"Going through the divorce was very difficult in itself, but it was also difficult within the Mennonite church. At the same time, there was a small group of people from First Deaf and the wider Mennonite church who were very supportive of me.

"Lester and Lois Brubaker from First Deaf have been with me throughout the whole experience. They stepped in and became my surrogate parents and grandparents for my kids. They had been close to both Don and me since we moved here and really grieved when he left. They showed me true support in every part of my life.

"The separation and divorce were things our church had to work through as well, not just me. Right after Don left, First Deaf set up a counsel group who worked with me from day one. Four years later, we still meet about every four months. No matter where life takes me, the people in that group will always be very special and important to me. They didn't just tap me on the shoulder and say, 'I'll pray for you.' They actually stuck their necks out and made decisions for me when I couldn't or when I was too emotionally upset to make a good decision. They counseled me on whether or not I should sign the divorce papers, whether I should go for child support through the state Youth and Family Services rather than waiting for Don, whether after the divorce was final it was okay for me to feel that I was a free person, whether, if I chose to, I could date and eventually remarry. The small group, and later the whole congregation at First Deaf, worked with me through all of that.

After the divorce was finalized, the church asked me to allow them to work through the issues of dating and remarriage after divorce. I didn't come up with the idea. In one way it felt good that they were looking ahead and, in a practical way, looking out for my interests more than I could. At the same time, I couldn't see that far ahead, and it was embarrassing to have my future placed before the entire congregation. Members of the congregation actually had to fill out papers stating whether, with the divorce finalized, they could accept me as a true sister in the Lord and allow me to participate fully as a member of First Deaf Mennonite. The paper also asked if they could free me to date and go on with my life in that way if I chose to. The large majority said yes, which was quite affirming. I know it was a struggle for some people to come to that decision. I was glad that they didn't just give a glib answer, but really searched.

"Even though people signed the statement and were sincere, I think it has taken a lot of them more than a year to put into practice what they said they felt. An example of that is when Eliza was 13, she was to meet with the elders. All the kids do at that age, to talk about their spiritual journeys. Eliza wasn't sure she wanted to do that and kept postponing it. I asked her why. What she told me, she also told the elders when she finally met with them. 'Well Mom, Don's been gone for two years, and the only people from church who have invited us to their house are Lois and Lester Brubaker. When I felt like we needed them most, they weren't there.' That is slowly changing. In the last six months more people from the church have included us in their lives.

"Some people needed time, and I can accept that. Now, after going through a kind of grieving process, they can invite me in. The fact that Don is remarried was an important factor for a small number of people in the congregation. They are able to release me now."

When another married couple at First Deaf separated, Sue was asked to be a member of a counsel group like the one the church set up for her. "When the elders asked me to be in the group, I felt I couldn't say no; it was something I felt I needed to do. I wanted to be there for them and do whatever I could in hopes that they would find reconciliation.

"I think people in the wider Mennonite church need to be more sensitive to members of their congregation who are going through divorce. The church at large makes it almost impossible for you to come forward and say you need help before you get to a crisis point. One couple told me that they hadn't slept in the same bedroom for nine years, but no one knew it. They were afraid to say they needed help. We make it hard for people to reach out and get help before it's too late, because we judge them. We make them feel like they're less than we are. That's an area we really need to work on. We also need resources available for people who are separated and divorced. It bothered me that there wasn't a Mennonite support group for me to go to, so I went to a Catholic support group.

"A lot of people have helped me after the separation and divorce. I started a new job in a Mennonite office right after Don left. My work supervisor, LaMar, guided me through many crises in that first tough year. When my mom died, LaMar and his wife Kass took off work and came to New Jersey for her funeral. I was away from home for several days, finalizing things with my family. It was August, and I hadn't done any lawn work for two weeks. I had no emotional or physical strength to take care of it before leaving for the funeral. It nagged at the back on my mind while I was in New Jersey. When I returned, to my surprise, everything was done. Not only had LaMar and Kass come to the funeral, but they had mowed my one-and-a-half acre yard and weeded all my flower beds.

"About a year ago my washer broke down and was not worth repairing. I didn't say much about it, although I knew I couldn't replace it because of my financial situation. I was going to the laundromat at six in the morning and coming to work at seven. Not many people knew that, but LaMar did. After a month or so he asked me, 'Are you still doing your laundry in the morning?' I told him yes. Well, LaMar called my pastor and found out about a man in my church who runs an appliance business. I got a call from him asking me when they could deliver my new washer.

"Mim Wert, who goes to First Deaf and is also my neighbor, sometimes runs my kids places and does things I can't do because I'm not able to be in two places at once. When I least expect it, Mim makes us supper. She totally surprises me. She'll call the kids when they get home from school and then brings it up. I come home from work and supper is made. She doesn't forget. Even though it's been four years since Don left, those things still happen.

"A Mennonite neighbor and friend, Naomi Carper, takes care of the kids if they're sick and I can't leave work. A man from church repairs my car, even if I can't pay him for awhile.

"Recently some friends from Alpha, New Jersey, came to visit. They know that I've had a constant struggle with finances, but they don't know when my needs are the greatest. On the way out the door, they handed me a large cash gift.

"For the kids it is a twofold thing. They are pleased, but we talk about how hard it is to receive. I don't want them to feel bad or inferior. They don't want to feel needy. At the same time, we are much better off than we were when Don left. I tell them that we're making it, and I try to stress that we weren't always this way. Now the Lord's looking after us. We don't have extras, but we have good food to eat, nice clothes, a car that runs, and we have our house. They appreciate that.

"At this time in my life I'm not equipped to give financial gifts to others. I am able to be there for someone who is hurting, or to share a meal. We joined the Names Project which helps people with AIDS. I took the kids to see the AIDS quilt at the university. I feel that we can give our time helping with projects like this.

"We weren't planning to be with extended family at Thanksgiving last year, so we called different agencies for unwed mothers and offered to host two girls whose families wouldn't have them for the holiday. The women who came each had little girls, and my kids loved the babies. We had a really good time. The one girl has reconciled with her family now, and the other is living on her own. We would like to have her back for Easter and in the summer for a picnic.

"I can still hear my father say, 'The ground at Calvary is level.' The love of Christ is offered to everybody—it's not exclusive. Because of Christ loving me, how can I not love someone else? That philosophy has influenced me to reach out to people of other races and people who are different because of their physical abilities, mental abilities, economic status, religious status, or sexual preference. I feel that we should accept each other for who we are and help each other because we want to help, not because we feel someone is less than we are or because it makes us feel good. I am grateful to the people who have shared with me in this way."

Sowing the Seed

(for Ardean Goertzen)

You never preached to me,
never told me about Jesus,
but when you took me—
divorced, grieving, broken—
into your home;
gently held me when I sobbed
on your couch;
rocked me in your arms,
listening far into the night;
you showed me
Jesus,
planted deep the seed
of His love,
made me ripe for Him.

Burt Kolinsky
Portland, Oregon

Accepted By Strangers

"My high school English teacher was my first contact with Mennonites," Janet Main remembers. "Her classes were so full of life. It was obvious that her faith was important to her, but she didn't talk about faith in the way I was used to. It showed in the way she related to students and in her teaching."

As a teenager, Janet thought she would be a pastor. Role models like her English teacher fueled the fires of that ambition, but, when she told her minister about her plans, he told her a woman couldn't be a pastor.

After high school, Janet longed to attend seminary but found no support in her congregation. So, she earned a Christian Education degree. After graduation she married a fellow student, and they accepted a two-year mission term in an isolated community in Manitoba. Although Janet had more pastoral leadership skills than her husband, they were overlooked because of her gender, and her husband was given sole responsibility of pastoral leadership. This situation caused conflict between them, and they were too isolated to find the support required to reconcile their conflict. Later, they moved to nearby Brandon to pursue further education and attempt to work at their relationship in a new setting. Shortly after the move their daughter Rebekah was born, but things only got worse.

The marriage eventually dissolved and Janet decided to stay in Brandon. She attended a Presbyterian church, where her best friend was the minister's wife. "I had the support of the pastoral couple and several individuals, but not the congregation. The congregation didn't even acknowledge that I was living through the anguish of a broken marriage."

When the divorce was finalized, Janet returned to her home community in Kitchener, Ontario. She maintained her goal of studying for the ministry but put it on the back burner and focused on daily survival for herself and Rebekah. Meanwhile, she searched for a church that would stimulate her intellectually and spiritually.

Then, through her job, she met Michael. He had also experienced a difficult marital breakup. She first befriended him to offer a listening ear, but came to enjoy his companionship and found they had a lot in common. As their friendship became more serious, she told him of her commitment to being involved in a church. Although Michael was not active in a church, he said that he would like to see what a Mennonite church was like. Janet contacted her former teacher to ask whether they would be welcome in her congregation. She told Janet they would be very welcome to come to Stirling Avenue Mennonite Church where she and her husband were members.

Members of the church received Janet and Michael warmly. The content of the worship service and the lifestyles of the church members fit with their expectations for a congregation. The service combined intellectual stimulus with faith and social action. But the pastoral team, which included both a man and a woman, was what appealed most to Janet.

"Vernon Leis and Mary Mae Schwartzentruber were relatively new pastors at the time, and were full of new ideas. To have a woman in the pulpit was especially meaningful to me," Janet recalls.

"One of the first things we got involved with at the church was a storytelling group led by Vernon. Twenty adults from diverse backgrounds met during the Sunday School hour. We gathered for 20 weeks so that each of us could tell our life story and have some feedback. We really bonded with that group of people. I had never shared so deeply with a group of strangers. Divorce was part of Michael's and my story, so we were straight and clear about that. I wondered if these people could accept us, knowing we were divorced and were hoping to marry each other. We were received warmly and compassionately without judgment.

"I felt like we had a rebirth and a fresh start together. We decided to be married at Stirling Avenue and invited the whole congregation to be our guests.

"Many older people in the congregation really embraced us.

No one ever said, 'This really gives me a problem that you are divorced and remarried.' "

The pastors at Stirling Avenue welcomed Janet's and Michael's talents and skills and invited them to become involved. Janet finally had opportunities to fulfill her teenage goal. This was the first church where she could freely exercise her leadership skills. In return, the church benefited from her contributions. Janet was chairperson of the Board of Christian Education for several years. Later, she served as deacon, enabling her to work with many people in the church through visitation and short-term projects which she organized. Michael was part of the congregation's Mission Ministry for six years.

In addition, Janet started other small storytelling groups similar to the one in which she and Michael had earlier participated. The groups provided an environment where different people could feel accepted and acceptable in the church. They were especially meaningful to women, just as Vernon Leis' group had been instrumental in Janet's involvement at Stirling Avenue.

"I think it is essential in the church to have groups that are nonthreatening, where people can tell their stories and share deeply. Maybe the whole church doesn't know their entire story, but that small support group knows, accepts, and cares.

"Because of my history of separation and divorce, and my struggles to be involved in church leadership, I found I could relate well to people who were experiencing similar difficulties. I was part of a women's group at Stirling Avenue. One woman in the group was going through a separation with her spouse, which was inconceivable to her. I tried to be supportive of her, because of my similar experiences.

"Another young woman came to the clothing center and was curious about the church. Mary Mae asked if I would drive the woman and her children to church and Sunday school. She was from Roman Catholic background and was going through a marital breakup. I walked with her during that time and when she discovered that her husband had sexually abused her children during visitations. I accompanied her to court hearings and helped her get established in a new home following the separation. I took her to a lot of second hand stores that I had discovered during my first years on my own. We found furniture for her apartment and clothing for her children.

"She told her story in a small group, and the people responded well to her and enjoyed her. But she didn't feel at home in the church. She didn't have much education past high school. The church consisted of well educated professional people, and it was hard for her to feel part of that group. It made me sad that people from different walks of life couldn't feel comfortable at our church.

"The church started a class for new attenders. It gave these people support, but didn't allow them much contact with the broader congregation. I participated in that class. Some of the people were abused as children or went through horrific divorces. The group became important to these hurting people, and they came every Sunday. It was one part of the church where they could fit in. When Michael and I invited the group to our home, one of the women said, 'Wow, this is church? I've never experienced this before.' "

Because of her deep fulfillment in varied forms of ministry at Stirling Avenue, Janet decided to continue training for pastoral ministry and enrolled in a ministerial course at a local Mennonite college. She incorporated her ideas about the usefulness of storytelling groups into a term paper about ministering to women. Janet gave her own story, reflecting on the pain of her divorce and the struggles she faced as a woman seeking leadership in the church. Janet also told about her joy in exercising her gifts at Stirling Avenue. Her story laid the groundwork in the paper for how a church can minister to people, with a special emphasis upon establishing small groups for sharing and support.

Janet wrote, "Sharing stories takes courage. Anger is part of my story, and will be a part of many people's experiences. It is hurtful when stories are met with indifference or judgment in the church. The hardest part for me in sharing at Stirling Avenue was fear of judgment. These were good, kind people, and I wanted to be part of them. What if they couldn't accept me as a divorced and remarried person? But, instead of the judgment

I feared, I found affirmation, care, and healing. My husband and I felt embraced. We found a release and the chance of a new beginning."

Vernon Leis, her pastor and academic supervisor, supported of Janet's paper and told her it was gutsy. But Janet's professor gave her a poor grade. Vernon arranged a meeting between Janet and the professor to discuss the paper and resolve the issues between them.

"My professor couldn't deal with the anger and painful aspects of my essay. Apparently he hadn't heard enough similar stories to mine and didn't know enough about where I was coming from."

Although Janet never did feel completely heard or understood by the professor, he did raise her grade after requiring her to rework some of the paper's content. Vernon continued to be supportive to her and said she was courageous to write such a paper.

This classroom experience showed Janet that not all Mennonites were like the members of Stirling Avenue. She learned that, like other denominations, the Mennonite church includes a wide variety of beliefs and perspectives.

Several years later differences surfaced at Stirling Avenue and caused conflict within the congregation. Mary Mae, one of the pastors who was extremely influential to Janet, resigned due to lack of support from male leaders, although the majority of the congregation supported her. Janet took part in efforts to resolve differences, but no reconciliation occurred. Janet is not attending the church anymore. However, she hopes that she can again find a place as meaningful and spiritually fulfilling as Stirling Avenue was to her for almost 10 years during the pastoral leadership of Mary Mae and Vernon.

Paul and Pat Sangree sampled a variety of denominations before joining the Mennonite church. They experienced the openness of the Unitarians, the peace emphasis of the Quakers, and the praise and worship of the charismatics. But they were not fully satisfied. "Although I appreciated the expressions of joy in the charismatic movement, I began to realize that joy in the morning, joy in the afternoon, and joy in the evening is not all there is to the Christian life," Pat reflected. "I thought there must be something more. Then the Lord showed us this group of people called Mennonites."

The Sangrees began attending the Gingrich Mennonite Church, Lebanon, Pennsylvania, after having become acquainted with the pastors, Abe Hoover and John Landis. Paul said, "Even though most of the members were dressed in plain attire, we never felt pressured to dress that way, and we found gracious acceptance." Pat emphasized, "There was so much love there that those little things didn't seem to intrude." Paul added, "I observed that the Mennonite denomination was in transition and I hoped that sooner or later they would drop those costumes and dress normal. And that's what has happened."

The Sangrees didn't hear a single sermon on peace and nonviolence during their time at Gingrich. "However," Paul observed, "it just seemed to flow with what we were experiencing. I never had any sense of being forced into a peace mind-set. The congregation's loving acceptance of us was significant in our coming to see the way of peace as intrinsic to the Gospel."

Within a year after becoming members at Gingrich, the Sangrees were invited to be pastor couple at the Schubert Mennonite Church, a small congregation nearby. They agreed to serve in team with the senior pastor. But on the day of their commissioning, the pastor resigned. Although they were totally unprepared for this, they decided to accept the challenge and do their best as relatively new members in the Mennonite church.

"To show you how absolutely green we were," Paul recalls, "I knew nothing about the Mennonite practice of men greeting one another with 'the holy kiss.' I would shake hands with the men and kiss the women. Well, it wasn't long until the deacon gently tapped me on the shoulder and said, 'Brother Sangree, you've got it backwards. Here at Schubert we men kiss the men and shake hands with the women.'"

Paul and Pat served at Schubert for six years. The same quality of love and acceptance that had drawn the Sangrees to the Gingrich Mennonite Church was characteristic of the Schubert congregation. Many people from the community came into the church, and the congregation grew from an average attendance of approximately 40 to over 100.

A Congregation's Transformation

South Christian Street is a narrow residential street in Lancaster's Seventh Ward—an economically disadvantaged part of the city. Harsh contrasts appear when one crosses into this area from the refurbished historical Old Town. The row houses fall into varied states of disrepair. The broken windows of some buildings stare vacantly, while others are curtained and homey. In the heart of the Seventh Ward sits an unpretentious brick building that houses a remarkable congregation.

South Christian Street Mennonite Church began as a Lancaster Mennonite Conference mission outreach in 1933 and has evolved into a congregation where its multi-cultural members work together to meet each other's needs, take part in leadership, and participate in home group fellowships.

The neighborhood surrounding the church was, and still is, a largely African-American and Hispanic community. In early years, relationships between the church's leaders, the congregation, and the community were divided by socioeconomic, geographic (rural versus urban), and racial differences.

"South Christian Street Mennonite was a church that did a lot of good things, like paying rent and buying shoes," Pastor Lawrence Chiles says. "But the congregation did not know how to reach these people or effectively minister to them because they could not identify with the kind of people who live here."

Church founders looked at the community members as their mission. In return, the residents looked to the church for help with finances, food, and clothing. Giving between the church and neighborhood people was largely one way, with the church trying to provide a solution to one problem until the next crisis arose. The church leadership had good intentions, but their disbursements encouraged dependency rather than providing a means by which individuals could help themselves.

"A lot of Mennonite churches in urban settings have never had African-American or Hispanic pastors. I'm the first here," says Lawrence. "We have quite a few people in the congregation who were used to the white pastors coming in with big cars and giving them corn and potatoes and that kind of thing. However, those things kept a number of the people here. Now they struggle with me. I don't have a long Buick and a farm, but I have a mouth and a heart that says we can work together."

Since his appointment at South Christian Street six years ago, Lawrence has worked with members to transform the church's methods of helping. "Our leadership team has agreed that we will not give aid unless people are willing to work with us. We cannot just hand out money to each person who asks. There are too many people that are in need in this particular quadrant of this city. The majority of the people are struggling to make ends meet. You can see the problems sitting on their shoulders.

"Instead of giving people money to meet their need (which may be very legitimate), our method is to work together with the person to address the problem. We may help them find employment. Or if they need education, we team together with them and find learning centers where they can train to get a job. There is tremendous reward when we work together like that. It is aid, but it is truly mutual.

"We had a Kenyan woman who was studying at a local college. She was asked to discontinue her studies because she could not meet her tuition payments. A mission agency in Africa was supposed to provide funds for her schooling but didn't do it.

"The congregation got together and said, 'How can we be sisters and brothers together to meet this need?' Different people agreed to do different things to help. One family let her stay in their home for a year. Another supplied her food. Several people formed a committee to work at the finances and help pay her debt. Others said they would help her find work. We decided together how to help this sister.

"That was a year ago. The original debt was $8,000, and our latest report from the college showed that we now owe $207.62. It may sound like our church has a lot of money. We don't.

Different people worked together, and she cooperated with our plan. She worked at our community center, Arbor Place, as a volunteer, and the church agreed to pay her $6.00 an hour which would go toward the college bill. We worked with the college and asked if they could match any money we sent. They agreed.

"When we did some renovations at the church we decided to tithe a set amount of money per volunteer hour and put it into a kitty for a needy cause. The kitty accumulated $2,000. Someone suggested we use $1,000 of it for the college debt, which we did. The college matched this to make a total of $2,000.

"She's working out fine at Arbor Place. She took off a year of school because the college wouldn't allow her to continue until the debt was paid. She will return next fall and get working papers. She cooperated. We worked together."

Today, the congregation at South Christian Street is racially and ethnically diverse. In addition to Lawrence's leadership, a team of black, white, and Hispanic members offer direction for worship services, youth programs, and home groups. The mix of languages, cultures, and races provides a setting for harmony, but also dissonance.

"We have found that when different cultures come together, each has stereotypes of the other. It is just like two magnets that repel each other. Difficult problems and misunderstandings develop until the magnets are turned around. Then they stick together.

"I believe that hanging together, in spite of all the tearing up and damage that occurs between us, is mutual aid. We have Nigerians, Kenyans, Dominicans, Puerto Ricans, African-Americans, and whites. It's a challenge, but it's the kind of church I have always wanted to pastor. Sometimes it feels like I am running around with a fire truck, trying to put out three different fires at once. That is why developing leadership is imperative. I can't pastor alone. In fact, if we don't develop leaders, it will be the downfall of the church.

"By developing leaders and encouraging people to use their gifts, the line between leader and lay person is blurred. Through participation in a home group fellowship, each person has opportunity to lead discussion, share and help solve problems, and give encouragement to other members of the group. The groups were organized by geographical location around the city, and meet weekly. When a crisis occurs, an individual has a support system within close proximity.

"The purpose of the home groups is to develop people. A number of individuals in this congregation have been here for many years and have never participated in any church responsibilities. They were just the recipients. We want to develop the gifts of all our people and help them realize that they can do things.

"Another goal is to help people fit in. Many people come into the church and show interest but don't know anyone. We try to connect new people with the home group in their neighborhood. That smaller group becomes a micro-church to them. Conversation starts and they get to know each other. When they come to church on Sunday they have familiar people to sit with, and the people in their home group introduce them to other members of the congregation."

The church is intentional about nurturing its young people. "Our mission is to reach the community kids. We can't reach them all—only a few. There are guys waiting out there like sharks to get our girls pregnant. We've worked hard at some of the sharks too.

"Our youth pastor, Vincent Whitman, and I got to know a young Haitian man. He was involved in drugs and crack right next door. Vincent and I began meeting with him. Now he attends the church and is part of a home group fellowship. His children had been taken away by the Child and Youth Services. All the children are now back, and the whole family is coming to church. A family from the congregation lives next to them and has taken them under their wing, working with them throughout the week. It doesn't happen quickly, but it is exciting to see the changes that can happen in people 's lives."

The congregation has helped many of its young people attend college. They hope the students will return to the church and contribute their skills to other youth. "We have a young man we worked with for years and years that we sent to Goshen College. We're very excited about that. Several elderly ladies in our church love to write letters to him and send him the Sunday bulletin. He's had his struggles, but he is determined to finish. Before he left this fall he asked me if I thought he could make it. I told him I did."

Glossary

Amish (page 30)—The most conservative group of Mennonites, who are distinguishable by their careful allegiance to the Bible and their *Ordnung,* the highly disciplined guidelines by which they live. Well known for their identifiable clothing, caution about modern conveniences, horse-drawn transportation, and practice of nonresistance.

Anabaptist (page 3)—The word means "to rebaptize." It was used in the sixteenth century to identify the group of reformers who insisted that persons who were baptized as infants be re-baptized as adults upon their own confession of faith in Jesus Christ. Mennonites practice adult baptist and are, therefore, one of the denominational groups known as Anabaptists.

Anointed (page 33)—A practice based on the biblical teaching found in James 5:14: "Is any one of you sick? He should call the elders of the church to pray over him and anoint him with oil in the name of the Lord."

Brethren in Christ (page 50)—An Anabaptist denomination having close ties with the Mennonite Church in doctrine and practice. The group originated about 1780 along the Susquehanna River in PA and was hence known as River Brethren (a name preserved by a conservative branch of the group.) Most of the first members were of Mennonite background.

Foot-washing (page 53)—A practice based on the biblical teaching found in John 13:1-17. Jesus washed his disciples' feet and taught them to do likewise. Traditionally, Mennonites have practiced footwashing in conjunction with communion, symbolizing their commitment to humility and service.

"Guess Who's Coming to Dinner"(page 86)—The practice in which members of a church (or other organization) volunteer to either host a meal in their home or go as guests to such a meal. Planners assign hosts and guests, and neither know in advance with whom they are matched.

Head Covering/Covering (page 142)—Cloth headgear worn by some Mennonite women in response to the biblical teaching in I Corinthians 11:1-16 that says a woman is to have her head covered when she prays.

Holdeman (page 38)—A conservative Mennonite group that originated in Wayne County, Ohio, in 1859, led by John Holdeman. It started as a protest against a perceived low level of spiritual life in the Mennonite church.

Holy Kiss (page 175)—A practice based on the biblical teaching found in I Corinthians 16:20: "Greet one another with a holy kiss." Mennonites have interpreted this to mean that men are to greet men and women are to greet women with a kiss of peace.

Mennonite Central Committee/MCC (pages 4, 49)—MCC is the major service and relief agency for the Mennonite and Brethren in Christ denominations with headquarters in Akron, Pennsylvania. MCC started in 1920 in response to famine and poverty among Mennonites in Russia.

Mennonite Disaster Service (page 4)—A service agency of the Mennonite Central Committee that helps meet cleanup and rebuilding needs resulting from natural disasters such as floods and hurricanes.

Relief Sale (page 51)—Various Mennonite communities across the United States and Canada sponsor relief sales, the proceeds of which are given to Mennonite Central Committee. The most popular items at these sales are the hand-stitched quilts made by Mennonite and Amish women.

Sewing circles (page 4)—Women's groups in the Mennonite church that sew clothing and prepare bedding for the poor.

Small group (pages 15, 56)—A small group of people within individual congregations or from other settings who gather regularly to provide spiritual and emotional support for one another. Many of these groups spend time studying the Bible and praying together.

Index

About the Authors

Glen A. Roth is a native of Albany, Oregon, and currently resides in Lancaster, Pennsylvania.

He has had a variety of careers within the Mennonite church—teacher and principal at Western Mennonite High School, teacher in Somalia, staff person with the Mennonite Board of Education, and pastor of East Chestnut Street Mennonite Church.

Currently he is Director of Education and Church Relations for Sharing Programs.

Sue V. Schlabach, Plymouth, Vermont, grew up in Perkasie, Pennsylvania.

She has worked as an advocate for victims of domestic violence at the Elkhart County (IN) Women's Shelter and as a graphic artist and writer for Sharing Programs.

Presently she is a free-lance writer and small-scale farmer.